William Beckford

FRONT ENDPAPER St Michael's Gallery, Fonthill Abbey
ABOVE Beckford's coat of arms as shown on the title page
of Rutter's *Delineations of Fonthill* (1823)
BACK ENDPAPER The Scarlet Drawing Room,
Lansdown Tower by Willes Maddox
TITLE PAGE An engraving after John Buckler's
Fonthill in Ruins (1825)

William Beckford

JAMES LEES-MILNE

COMPTON RUSSELL

Photographic Acknowledgments

Boyd Alexander Esq., 39. Collection of the Duke of Atholl, Blair Castle (photo. Scottish National Portrait Gallery), 21. Barber Institute of Fine Arts, University of Birmingham, 87. Bath Reference Library, 7-1. The Rt. Hon. The Lord Mayor of Bristol, Councillor Hubert J. Williams, 62. The British Architectural Library, Royal Institute of British Architects, 53, 81, 82. Trustees of the British Museum, 95. Country Life, 61, 78, 84, 88, 89, 103. Edmund Esdaile, Esq., 75. John Everingham, 83, 115. The Duke of Hamilton & Brandon, 17, 70. John Harris, Esq., 49. The Earl of Harrowby, 29. Controller of Her Majesty's Stationery Office, 12. The Henry E. Huntingdon Library & Art Gallery, 30. Ironmongers' Hall (photo. Country Life), 60. Trustees of the Lady Lever Art Gallery, Port Sunlight, 19. Jon Millington, half title, title, 12, 15, 26, 27, 46, 48, 50, 51, 52, 54, 61, 62, 63, 64, 67, 68, 69, 85, 86, 90, 119. Derry Moore, Endpapers, 26, 44, 85, 102, 109, 120. Morrison Estates (photo. Humphrey Stone), 14. Mozart's Birthplace, Salzburg, 20. The Trustees, The National Gallery, London, 57, 94, 97, 99, 101. National Portrait Gallery, London, 22, 24, 28, 59. The National Trust, Anglesey Abbey, 100. The National Trust, Charlecote, Warwickshire, 65, 66. The National Trust, Scotland, 113. The National Trust, for Scotland, Brodick Castle, 58, 71, 116, 117. The National Trust, Stourhead, 96. The National Trust, Upton, 23. Radio Times Hulton Picture Library, 22. Neil Rimington, 47 (photo. Professor John Wilton-Ely) 90 (photo. Michael Campbell). Royal Commission on Historical Monuments, 14, 65. Royal Institute of British Architects, Drawings Collection, Back Cover, 42. Salford Art Gallery, 74. Sotheby's, 104. Humphrey Stone, 76. Peter Summers, Esq. 16. Victoria & Albert Museum, Crown copyright, Front cover, 37, 48, 49, 66, 91. The Trustees of the Wallace Collection, 38.

© James Lees-Milne 1976
First published in Great Britain 1976 by
COMPTON RUSSELL LTD
The Old Brewery, Tisbury, Wiltshire
Designed by Humphrey Stone
and filmset in Apollo
Printed offset by BAS Printers Limited,
Wallop, Hampshire
All rights reserved
ISBN 0 85955 036 2

CONTENTS

Preface   7

1 Gilded Boyhood   11

2 Tarnished Youth   25

3 Portuguese Summer   31

4 Fonthill Abbey   41

5 Stucco Halls   60

6 Lansdown: A Famous Landmark   77

7 Bath: Lansdown Crescent   95

8 Winter of Discontent   112

  Bibliography   123

  Index   125

PREFACE

'How strange my make-up is! The working of my brain is enough to perplex anyone wanting to know about the composition of the human spirit!' Who was this strange, self-analytical being? And of what importance is he to us? William Beckford's chief claims to remembrance have till very recently been confined to his composition of the oriental tale *Vathek,* his building of Gothic Fonthill Abbey and his eccentricities of one sort and another. True, he was a millionaire which allowed him to be a spendthrift, but as *The Times* newspaper of 6th July 1822 put it, 'He was one of the very few possessors of great wealth who have honestly tried to spend it poetically.' True, he was also a sexual deviant, which quirk of nature was during the age he lived in a distinct social disadvantage. To a large extent it determined his peculiar character and gave a keen edge to his sensibilities, as the ensuing pages may indicate. To Elizabeth Lady Craven, who inquired what were the reasons for his retiring and savage disposition, he wrote, at the age of thirty-three, what he could well have written half a century later:

I have been hunted down and persecuted these many years. I have been stung and lacerated and not allowed opportunities of changing that snarling, barking style you complain of, had I ever so great an inclination. If I am shy or savage you must consider the baitings and worryings to which I allude – how I was treated in Portugal, in Spain, in France, in Switzerland, at home, abroad, in every region . . .

treated, let it be clearly understood, not by foreigners, but by his own countrymen, and in particular by people of his own class.

Beckford was a man of parts in the eighteenth-century sense of that word. To the eighteenth century he belonged—his best creative work was conceived before 1800—whereas he was endowed with the mind of a nineteenth-century intellectual. Without undue exaggeration we may say that he possessed the attributes of the universal man. He judged causes and events as a cosmopolitan. He was trilingual in English, French and Italian, besides speaking Spanish, German, Portuguese, Persian and Arabic. His exceeding cleverness was acknowledged by his con-temporaries. When he was a child of seven his tutor wrote of his 'extraordinary abilities'; and the architect James Wyatt echoed these very words after first meeting him in 1794. Someone who knew him in his old age wrote, 'I believe he was one of the most keen-sighted men that ever lived. He fathomed human character and looked into a man's soul in a moment . . .' He said, 'Men's faces are a sort of alphabet to me; I can read their minds as easily as I can read a book.' For critical acumen, descriptive power and sheer wit his writing approximates to that of two famous European poets a generation older and younger than himself, namely the Italian Vittorio Alfieri and the Englishman Lord Byron. Beckford, who after all must rank in history first and foremost as a writer, can by virtue of the astonishing ebullience of his prose (and also the sad heaviness of his verse) be termed a poet manqué. As a travel writer he is unsurpassed. Nothing that was beautiful or unusual escaped his eye. His readiness to applaud, denigrate and mock never failed him. Joseph Farington noted in his diary that throughout his writings 'there was a spirit like champagne prevailing—sparkling everywhere.' When he allowed his pen to range freely Beckford's prose was always diverting (not for example, like Horace Walpole's, contrived), devastatingly sharp and amazingly modern. Like Byron, Beckford antedated the sophisticated satire writers of recent times, Wilde, Firbank and Evelyn Waugh.

But there is more to Beckford than his incomparable prose and his unpredictable character. He was a collector of paintings, furniture, books, and works of art of every sort and description. He was patron on a lavish scale of contemporary artists and musicians. He was also of course a builder and, last but not least, a gardener and landscape designer of no mean order.

There exist several excellent biographies and many articles on the various aspects of William Beckford. From them I have drawn copiously. In a text of this exiguous length it seemed pedantic to acknowledge every reference made to them in a plethora of footnotes. Instead I have mentioned in the text the source of the most important, or contentious references, which is amplified in my Bibliography on page 123.

The authority to whom I am most indebted is, of course, Mr. Boyd Alexander. He knows more and has revealed more about Beckford than any man living. His books and articles are indispensable reading to anyone venturing upon Beckfordism.

There are many friends to whom I owe grateful thanks: John Jolliffe, for first suggesting that I should undertake this monograph; Brian Fothergill, Beckford's forthcoming biographer, for discussing with me the complexities of a common interest; Clive Wainwright, for putting me on to some abstruse articles about Beckford's collections; John Wilton-Ely, for giving me an extract from Farington's unpublished diaries about the proposed 'Revelation Chamber' in Fonthill Abbey; Anthony Hobson, for help and information regarding Beckford's library; Dr. Leslie Hilliard, for access to Lansdown Tower; Neil Rimington, for access to the remains of Fonthill Abbey; and Lady Margadale, for access to the Fonthill boathouse and the Morrison Papers. Above all I am grateful to Julian Berry, Michael Russell, and Jon Millington for diligently reading my typescript and making invaluable criticisms and suggestions. They must in no sense be held responsible for the use I have made of their labours.

This book is addressed to those people to whom William Beckford of Fonthill is merely a name. Its purpose is to point out briefly, with the help of illustrations, the significance of an extraordinary Englishman, whose type once fairly familiar in the social scene, is now extinct.

J. L-M.

BATH

0   5   10   15
Miles

Trowbridge

Warminster

Hindon

Wilton

• Fonthill

SALISBURY

The relationship of Fonthill to Salisbury and Bath

A map of WILLIAM BECKFORD'S Estate at FONTHILL showing it approximately as it was in his lifetime

Berwick St Leonard

Fonthill Bishop

Ridge Farm

Hindon

Lodge Gateway

Site of SPLENDENS

Little Ridge Wood

Ridge Hill

THE TERRACE

Stop Farm

Lower Street Gate

Knap Farm

Lower North Terrace

Higher North Terrace

Fonthill Gifford

Alpine Gardens

Quarry Wood

TERRACE

Hodway Hanging

Newclose Hanging

Clerks Walk

Fonthill Abbey Ruins

Jenny's Corner Gate

Birch Boll Gate

Ashleywood Farm

Vicarage Barn

Knoyle Corner

Kennimer Hanging

Great Western Avenue

Bitham Lake

American Gardens

Fonthill Stream

Ruddlemoor Farm

Bottom Copse

Stone Gate

Fonthill Abbey Wood

Pine Lawn

Lawn Lodge

Hillstreet Farm

Stop Beacon 700 ft.

Lower Lawn Farm

Norwegian Lawn

Rough Lawn

South End Gate

West Gate

White Mead Wood

Old Park

Higher Lawn Farm

Upper Lawn Cottages

TISBURY

Pyt House

Newtown

East Hatch

KEY
- - - - - The Ride
· · · · · The Walk
▬▬▬▬ The Wall

0   ¼   ½   ¾   1 Mile

Denys R. Baker

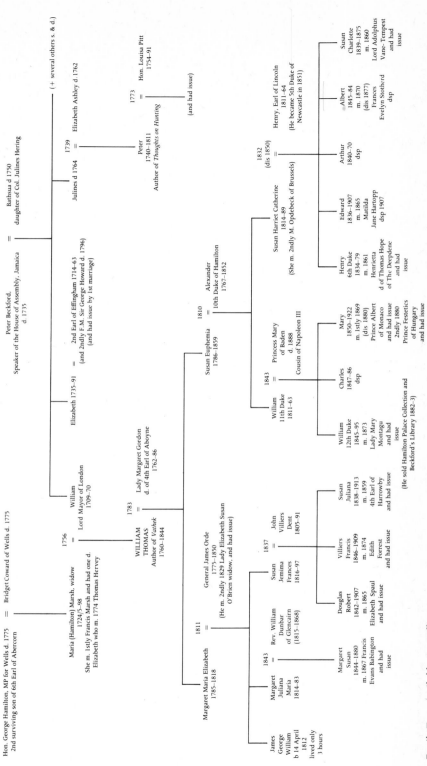

Family Tree compiled by Jon Millington

1 · GILDED BOYHOOD

ILLIAM Beckford was born with an outsize silver spoon in his mouth on 29th September 1760, less than one month before the sudden death of King George II. As a mere babe in arms he was carried by a paternal aunt, Lady Effingham, who was a Lady of the Bedchamber, into the royal presence at St. James's court. In later life he remarked that whereas his monarch saw him, he could not remember seeing his monarch. The child's antecedents were mixed. The Beckfords were parvenus but immensely rich. They were also a passionate and violent breed. The great-grandfather Peter Beckford was Governor of Jamaica where he amassed a fortune from sugar and slaves, and died in a brawl in 1711. His son, likewise Peter, became Speaker of the Jamaican Assembly. He was a rough diamond who in a rage stabbed to death the deputy Judge Advocate, a man twice his age. His brother Thomas was killed by a man whom he had offended. Speaker Peter died in 1735. His second son was William, known as Alderman Beckford, twice Lord Mayor of London, and the father of the subject of this book. The Alderman was educated at Westminster School, became a Whig M.P. notorious for his radical and outspoken views – he dared to rebuke George III to his face in a public speech – and about 1736 bought the Fonthill estate in Wiltshire.

In spite of an ugly Jamaican accent and uncouth manners the Alderman was a cultivated man with a taste for the arts, which his inordinate wealth enabled him to gratify. He earned the respect and friendship of his parliamentary colleague the great Lord Chatham, whom he persuaded to be young William's godfather. After the Alderman's death from a chill in 1770, Chatham found himself appointed by his friend's will one of the boy's guardians. Young William, fatherless at the age of nine, inherited a huge country house and estate in addition to capital of £1½ million and an annual income from Jamaica of £70,000. He was also left with a host of his father's impecunious and disputatious bastards older than himself (Horace Walpole said they numbered thirty, but the names of only six sons and one daughter have come down to us), a doting, but scolding mother, and a legitimate half-sister by his mother's previous marriage. Mrs. Beckford provided the patrician lineage of which her son was all his life inordinately proud. She was born Maria Hamilton, eldest daughter of the Hon. George Hamilton, M.P. for Wells, and granddaughter of the 6th Earl of Abercorn.

Beckford never quite escaped the shadow of his father's dominant personality. The commanding, virile and ruthless Alderman was portrayed, not unsympathetically, by the son as the fictitious Caliph Vathek and the Emir Abou Taher Achmed. His death so early in the son's

life was in many respects disastrous. He had been a formidable and in some respects an endearing parent, whom young William had held in awe and admiration. From the little we can glean of their relationship, the father would stand no nonsense from the boy's airs and graces, and would tease him by reminding him of his plebeian paternal ancestry. The more indignant young William became the more the father was amused.

From the Beckfords young William inherited wilfulness, petulance and an unbridled temper. But he totally lacked their masculinity. He was a delicate child, of feminine if not effeminate manner, extreme sensitivity and overwrought imagination. Alternately indulged and chastised by his apprehensive mother, the boy was not sent to school and led an isolated life without friends of his own age. Yet he received a first-rate education and showed an astonishing aptitude for learning. His first tutor, Robert Drysdale, a young Scot appointed in 1767, recorded that

He has been accustomed to speak and read French since he was 3 or 4 years old, and had begun the Latin a year before I came here. He is of a very agreeable disposition, but begins already to think of being master of a great fortune.

The setting of this lonely life was not the Fonthill House which the Alderman had bought, for that was burnt down in 1755, but the huge Palladian palace with which he had immediately replaced it. The bulky central block boasted a majestic portico approached by a double flight of balustraded steps and was connected by curved colonnades to a pair of handsome pavilions with cupolas. Its architect seems to have been an obscure London master-builder called James or George Hoare. Considering the closeness of Fonthill to Stourhead, the seat of the Hoare family, the master-builder may have had local connections. The site of the imposing structure, which the Alderman's neighbours christened Splendens, was at the bottom of a wooded valley on the west margin of an artificial lake, complete with bridge, grotto and unique boathouse, apsed and aisled like a rococo basilica in miniature. All these delights were created by the Alderman after 1736 together with a new classical church on a hill, a temple and a pagoda, which have long since disappeared.

The visitor approaching on the Salisbury-Hindon road would after passing through fairly desolate downlands enter this paradisal domain through an imposing arched gateway (which survives), reputedly designed by Inigo Jones but doubtless by the Alderman's master-builder Hoare. Descriptions of Splendens by contemporaries all paid tribute to its magnificence while hinting at touches of vulgarity. Mrs. Lybbe Powys in 1776 referred to the 'utmost profusion of magnificence' of the *piano nobile*, 'with the appearance of immense riches, almost too tawdrily exhibited. The chimneypieces all over the house are elegant to a degree . . . all of statuary or Siena marble.' Those carved by J. F. Moore which survive are indeed of the highest sculptural quality. Several ceilings were painted by Andrea Casali, a native of Civita Vecchia, with insipid deities. There were two apartments which particularly struck visitors as unusual, and which

OPPOSITE LEFT Alderman William Beckford (1709–70), father of the author of *Vathek*, in process of rebuilding Fonthill after the fire of 1755. By Tilly Kettle.

OPPOSITE RIGHT Mrs. Beckford (née Maria Hamilton), 'The Begum', Beckford's mother, in front of Fonthill Splendens, c. 1790. By Benjamin West.

OPPOSITE BELOW Fonthill Splendens, view from the north showing the huge Palladian house built on the west bank of the lake. It was demolished by Beckford in 1807. Engraving after J. M. W. Turner from W. Angus's *Seats* (1787).

William Beckford as a boy in Vandyke costume, with a whippet and spaniel. Probably by William Hoare.

A marble chimneypiece, carved by J. F. Moore, formerly in Splendens and now in the Manor House, Beaminster, Dorset.

had a profound effect on young William. They were the entrance hall and the Turkish Room, both on the ground floor. Mrs. Powys found the former dark and gloomy, which it undoubtedly was owing to paucity of windows, and a low vaulted roof supported by immense stone piers. It was eighty-five feet long (i.e. the entire width of the house) and known as the Egyptian Hall. Beckford said that it looked as though hewn out of the living rock and led into seemingly endless passages, also low and vaulted. It was the inspiration of the hall of Eblis in *Vathek*.

Entrance gateway to the park at Fonthill Bishop. Attributed to Inigo Jones, but probably built by Hoare for Alderman Beckford.

The other apartment was by contrast small and exotic. In *Illustrations of Fonthill Abbey* (1823) John Britton ('that highly ridiculous, highly impertinent Britton, the Cathedral fellow', as Beckford was to describe him) called the Turkish Room 'as splendid and sumptuous as those magical recesses of enchanted palaces . . . in the Arabian Nights entertainments'. Nor was this language extravagant. The coved ceiling was painted by F. J. Boileau (a protégé of the Duke of Orleans) with arabesques and flowers on a gold ground. The window shutters were of looking-glass which made the room seem boundless. Facing the windows the fireplace was, according to the Hon. Anne Rushout, a visitor in 1799, shut up in summer to resemble an altar of verde antique with grate-work of gilt bronze. Opposite the entrance door was a looking-glass down to the ground with orange drapery over it. A red-brown Persian carpet, orange silk window blinds, orange curtains fringed with gold, ottomans and plump floor cushions completed the air of oriental hedonism. This room, presumably decorated by the Alderman, had a lasting influence upon his son's love of all eastern things. In 1788 Beckford commissioned Soane to make a new picture gallery out of an attic passage, together with chimneypieces for the Tapestry Room and South-East Parlour, which were executed by the sculptors Banks, Flaxman and Bacon. In the 1790s James Wyatt made some improvements to the Library, the ceiling of which Anne Rushout noticed to be 'Gothic-ish'.

The oriental fantasies of Beckford's boyhood were fostered by one of the most mysterious artists of genius, Alexander Cozens. He was engaged by Mrs. Beckford (whom her son irreverently called the Begum) to teach him drawing. Born in Russia in 1717 Cozens first came to England in 1746. His father was not Peter the Great – though this notion of his pupil's was

Fonthill Splendens, the Palladian house with portico and wings rebuilt for Alderman Beckford after 1755 by James or George Hoare. From a plate in C. Hoare's *Modern Wiltshire*.

A plate with Chinese armorial design showing the arms of the Beckford family, c. 1750, from a service which probably belonged to Alderman Beckford.

too romantic to be discouraged – but one of the Czar's immigrant ship builders. Cozens fed the boy's imagination with tales of St. Petersburg, the gilded opulence of the city's inhabitants, the long winter nights and the jingling sleigh drives through illimitable snow. He introduced to him the writings of Ossian and *The Arabian Nights*. He shared with him a taste for magic (and quite possibly a touch of the black sort too). He encouraged his charge's belief that the Beckfords and Hamiltons were descended from a long line of kings. He won his entire confidence and retained it for many years. Most important, he encouraged the boy to write. At the age of seventeen Beckford, who looked upon Cozens as his mentor and guide, wrote *The Vision* for him, a story in which he identified Cozens with Moisasour, a sort of Mozartian high priest, 'who can read my inmost soul'. Cozens was, as A. E. Oppé remarked, 'one of the few who understood Beckford's reluctance to exchange his life of super-sensibility and poetic melancholy for the public activities into which he was being pressed by his family'.

The Begum did not at all favour her son's obsession with the orient and the occult, and wrote to tell Lord Chatham so. That statesman accordingly warned his godson, whom he wryly described as 'compounded of the elements of air and fire', against inordinate dabbling in Arabian fiction. And Beckford's idiotic new tutor, the Rev. John Lettice, persuaded his pupil to sacrifice a splendid heap of oriental drawings by burning them. Furthermore Mrs. Beckford was not at all sure that writing was quite the thing for a young gentleman whose forebears had long played a part in public affairs, and who was the possessor of the pocket borough of Hindon. When in 1780 her son actually published *Biographical Memoirs of Extraordinary Painters*, a skit provoked by his reading ridiculous criticisms of certain Dutch painters and overhearing the Fonthill housekeeper's ignorant prattle to visitors about his father's collections, she was not amused. Considering that Beckford was sixteen when he began writing them, the lives of Og of Basan, Watersouchy and Blunderbussiana are not particularly funny. The book does however emit occasional flashes of that wit of which Beckford was to become a master, as when he described a decapitated martyr with his head in his hands: 'The astonishment of the head at finding itself off its own shoulders was expressed to admiration and the attitude of the Blessed St. Denis as natural as that of any man, who ever carried such a burden.' *The Vision* (given that title when first published in 1930) was only a little more adult, 'a formless and monotonous piece, without action or culmination,' the *Times Literary Supplement* called it, 'a mere ramble through a spectral panorama of peaks, cliffs, lakes and caverns in some indeterminate Orient.' Yet, the reviewer went on, the young author already had 'full command of his luminous, marmorean style', which is more than can be said for Mrs. Radcliffe's comparable *The Mysteries of Udolpho*, which it preceded.

Before the *Biographical Memoirs* confronted an indifferent public the

Begum and a plethora of aunts, uncles and advisers decided that the boy should finish his education in Geneva, where, accompanied by the tutor Lettice, he arrived in the autumn of 1777. Immediately Beckford fell on his feet and profited to great advantage. He mastered with amazing facility Italian, Spanish, German and Portuguese. He consorted with philosophers and submitted himself to the tuition of some leading European intellects, notably François Huber, the naturalist, great authority on bees, noted agnostic and eccentric, and H. Bénédict de Saussure, one of the earliest Alpine explorers. He certainly met Voltaire once, if not more often. The great man granted him a formal reception at which he praised the Alderman's liberalism. Beckford was struck by the octogenarian's penetrating eyes. Throughout the year's absence from England he wrote regularly to Cozens. In one letter he hotly dissociated himself from the normal beer-swilling, sport-addicted English student in Switzerland, ending with the words, 'Such an animal I am determined not to be.' Unfortunately this is just what Mrs. Beckford thought he ought to be. Alarmed by reports from the Reverend Lettice of the perils to her son's soul in the company he kept, the methodistical matriarch rushed to Geneva to retrieve him for the benefit, as she fondly hoped, of English society and politics.

But Mrs. Beckford was too late. Her son's interests were already focused along unorthodox lines. Back at Fonthill young Beckford refused to hunt or shoot. This did not mean that he was not devoted to horsemanship: it merely meant that he would not kill for sport. Switzerland had confirmed his love of nature in every aspect, including the animal kingdom. All forms of cruelty to animals he abominated, whether hunting, shooting, bull-fighting or even fishing. He could not bear to see fishes gasping on the banks. To watch people with nets indiscriminately catching butterflies drove him to call them 'torturers'. He inveighed against the vivisection of dogs, and referred to the 'hellish Majendie's experiments upon the unoffending animals he submits to the most horrible and lingering torture'. He was overjoyed to discover that some lambs presented at an altar of a Portuguese monastery, instead of being sacrificed, were afterwards reared with tenderness. And when the old prior agreed with him that a cry of distress from the humblest beast was heeded by the Almighty, he almost embraced him. Moreover Beckford had an uncanny way with animals. It is related that once in the Paris zoo, to the alarm of the keepers, he entered the cage of a dangerous lioness, who allowed him to stroke her. She returned his caresses to the extent of licking off the skin of his fingers with her rough tongue.

Animals and birds were encouraged to proliferate within the Fonthill barrier. In 1799 Miss Rushout counted more than thirty swans on the lake. James Storer was amazed that the hares were tame enough to eat out of the human hand — at least Beckford's. And as for dogs Beckford was far happier in their company than in any human being's. Caroline and Spotty,

Viscount Fartleberry, one of Beckford's dogs. A drawing by the Abbé Macquin.

17

he wrote in 1812, 'are lovelier and more attractive than ever, and I adore them – a hundred times more than the other limited, chilly, touchy members of my family . . . Too much cannot be said for these animals. They show a gentleness, an affectionate tenderness that goes to my heart.' The eventual death of Caroline caused him the most intense anguish:

Never more will she appear sleeping at my feet; never more will she console me with those intelligent looks so full of affection for me. I feel as if there was a ball of lead in the pit of my stomach; there are painful constrictions in my forehead. Tears have not yet come to my aid . . .

The first visit abroad had set in motion Beckford's travel writing. In a series of letters, *An Excursion to the Grande Chartreuse in the Year 1778*, he described the appeal wild and savage nature had for him in the remote, mountainous Dauphiné. During the three days which he spent as guest of the Carthusian monks he also learnt to appreciate the rigorous blessings of claustral life, which he was to simulate in his own Fonthill Abbey. The hospitable fathers were captivated by their young visitor. When he told them he was owner of ruined Witham Abbey, Somerset, of which the third prior had been St. Hugh of Lincoln, their joy knew no bounds. St. Hugh had visited the Grande Chartreuse in the twelfth century. 'The Secretary, almost with tears in his eyes, beseeched me to revere these consecrated edifices for the sake of St. Hugo,' he wrote. It is perhaps worth mentioning that in 1783 Beckford became a warden of Witham Friary church.

In June 1779 he was sent, in the charge of the ubiquitous Lettice, on a tour of English country houses, to see whether it would not redirect his interests into conventional channels and those rural pursuits befitting his station in county circles. The result was even more disastrous than anything the Begum could possibly have conceived. An incident occurred which was to affect his whole life and character, to lead to social ostracism, persecution, loneliness and permanent discontent. At Powderham Castle on the delta of the river Exe he met and fell head over heels in love with Lord and Lady Courtenay's youngest child and only son, William, aged eleven. The tale has been dwelt upon too often to need re-telling in detail. Beckford was exalted at one moment to the skies, plunged the next into depths of despair. He confided his condition to the sympathetic ears of Alexander Cozens ('I grew sensible there was a pleasure in loving something besides myself'), and wrote passionate letters to William, 'little C', 'the little Dove'. Unwisely, as things turned out, he flaunted his love in the Courtenay and Beckford households. He also confided in the boy's aunt, Charlotte Courtenay, whose sentiments for Beckford were scarcely less warm than the nephew's. Hubris and euphoria were two besetting infirmities to which Beckford was not immune. And when the storm broke he was overtaken by the retribution which inexorably attends them. As for the homosexuality itself, André Parreaux sees in it a mixture of narcissism and nostalgia for the innocence of his lost childhood.

The Hon. William Courtenay (1768–1835), 'Kitty', later 3rd Viscount Courtenay and 9th Earl of Devon, with whom Beckford was involved in the scandal of 1784. Portrait painted for Beckford by George Romney, 1781.

Tearing himself away from Powderham Castle, or possibly being chivvied by the worried Mr. Lettice, Beckford accompanied his tutor to the English Lakes. His highly romantic description of their scenery antedates the praises of the nature poets, Wordsworth, Coleridge and Southey. He was in fact among the very first writers to appreciate the sublimity of natural scenery in the raw. He loved the English landscape as ardently as he detested its inhabitants; and he deplored its defacement by ill-judged building.

For me the monotony of all these houses which resemble each other like cherries, of all these little gardens and all these little Methodist chapels, etc. is tiresome in the highest degree. One can no longer find a single field, a single wood or a single green hill which isn't in the act of being transformed into battalions of houses — all built in straight lines, with their everlasting little roads of yellow sand bordered with cypress and laurel.

And again in justifiable protest against the ruthless scarring of the landscape by railway contractors and factory tycoons, he was to exclaim furiously (and alas, prophetically),

Il n'y a plus de campagne nulle part — on abat les forêts, on viole les montagnes . . . on se fiche des rivières — partout le gaz et la vapeur — la même odeur, les mêmes tourbillions d'exécrable fumée épaise et fétide.

He was far-seeing, too, in other ways. He foretold that doctors would within a century be honoured instead of ridiculed, and the prolongation of life would rank above the cure of souls; and even that cooks would be deemed socially acceptable! 'Every lady will be proud to marry her apothecary and every lord his cook maid.' He ventured to predict that 'every kind of exclusive system, reserved seats and pews . . . will be done away with. Universal toleration will produce in process of time not only universal suffrage, but universal simplicity of manners'; while bishops would cease to sit in the House of Lords and the clergy be obliged to live and work in their country parishes. This is the Beckford who long before the French Revolution was deploring exploitation of the working classes — without, it must be admitted, once questioning his right to own Jamaican slaves, a right which perfectly civilized people accepted before the abolition of slavery in 1796.

Alarmed by Lettice's reports Mrs. Beckford in desperation now invited to Fonthill her husband's nephew Peter Beckford, the future author of *Thoughts upon Hunting*, and his attractive wife Louisa, who might as a woman older than her too susceptible son distract him from his infatuation for the Courtenay boy. The Begum's excellent intentions were doomed again to worse than failure. Louisa fell madly in love with William who made her a willing accomplice in his pursuit of 'Kitty', as they referred to little C in their correspondence. The situation was to become more tangled than before. In a last vain attempt to steer her son into the straight and narrow path before he came of age, Mrs. Beckford

Louisa, daughter of 1st Lord Rivers and wife of Peter Beckford. She was infatuated with William Beckford, her husband's first cousin. She died of tuberculosis in 1791. Part of a portrait by Reynolds painted for Beckford, 1782.

19

despatched him, accompanied by watchdog Lettice, on a final grand tour of the Continent.

Before leaving London in June 1780 Beckford witnessed the Gordon Riots. The fires made a lasting contribution to his store of artistic impressions, and the savage sentences imposed upon the rioters by Alexander Wedderburn aroused in him feelings of deep hostility, intensified perhaps by his instantaneous sympathy for the underdog. He made his views on Wedderburn widely known.

The travellers passed through Holland. Beckford laughed at the Dutch whose flabby faces and oyster eyes resembled those of the fish from whom he fancied they were descended when the country was once under water. The party sailed south up the Rhine. They stopped at Mannheim – where Beckford admired the Elector's new architecture – at Vienna, Augsburg and Munich. Strangely enough he dismissed the rococo pavilions, Nymphenburg, Pagodenburg and Amalienburg, as 'all tinsel'. By August he had reached his goal, Italy. He found Venice a dying city of whose ancient beauties Canaletto had rendered all literary description superfluous. His father had collected at least one Canaletto painting for Splendens. In Venice he was introduced to two sisters and a brother of the Cornaro family. One sister fell in love with Beckford; and Beckford fell in love with the brother. 'One image alone possesses me and pursues me in a terrible way . . . This unique object is all I hope for – I am dead to everything else,' he confided to a Venetian acquaintance. He was tormented by guilt and confusion. In his diary of 26th October he jotted down, 'Think where I was this time [last] year, happy and sequestered with my love Wm.' Inconstancy then was another failing to reckon with. Life was full of perplexities, yet it was fun all the same. In Rome the diaries were filled with adolescent yearnings and moanings. In Naples he stayed with his kinsman Sir William Hamilton and his first wife Catherine, a talented harpsichord player with whom Beckford made music and to whom he became devoted.

Beckford had nourished a passion for music since childhood. At the age of five he had received lessons from Mozart, who was eight: 'poor dear Mozart' and 'that moonstruck, wayward boy' is how he used familiarly to describe this genius of all time. He maintained that during a lesson either he or Mozart (for he was to give alternative versions of the story) struck off the air 'Non più andrai', which Mozart subsequently introduced in the opera *Le Nozze di Figaro*. In a small way Beckford too was a composer, with a capacity for improvising that could astonish and delight the uninitiated. He played, we are not sure how well, the harpsichord. His favourite composers were Corelli, Haydn, Jommelli and Mozart, every one of whose operas he attended in London, score in hand, loudly hissing whenever a singer or the orchestra were at fault. In London at the age of twenty he made fast friends with the famous *castrato* Gasparo Pacchierotti, whom he met again in Lucca on his way from Venice to Rome

W. A. Mozart (1756–91), at approximately eight years old when he gave music lessons to Beckford, then aged five. Portrait by J. Zoffany painted in London, 1764–5.

20

and took for long rambles in the misty mountains to the detriment of the *maestro*'s vocal chords. He was to become no less intimate with F. G. Bertoni, a celebrated composer of opera, notably *Quinto Fabio* (beloved by Beckford) in which Bertoni's friend Pacchierotti sang at Drury Lane. He was also to enlist John Burton, the finest professional harpsichord player of the day, as his household musician. In Paris in 1784 he was to see a lot of Sacchini during the writing of the opera *Chimène*, and claimed to have composed for him the air 'Mon espoir s'est éteint et mon amour me reste'. From Naples he went out of his way to visit the septuagenarian Farinelli, another great *castrato*, who in the distant past had sung nightly to the melancholic King Philip V of Spain the same four songs for nearly twenty years. Beckford induced Farinelli to sing to his accompaniment. 'His modulation is still delightful and some of those thrilling tunes which raised such raptures in the year '35 have not yet entirely deserted him,' Beckford told a friend. 'The remembrance of a period when he was almost deified . . . made him burst into tears.' To soothe the old virtuoso the young man composed for him a Sicilian air.

B. J. Maslen, however, has questioned Beckford's musical skill and

Sir William Hamilton and his first wife, Catherine, in Naples. She became a confidante of Beckford.

21

Gasparo Pacchierotti (1744–1821), a famous *castrato*, from a caricature entitled *A Sunday Concert*, 1782, engraved by C. Loraine Smith.

A. M. G. Sacchini (1734–86), Neapolitan composer of the opera *Chimène* (and forty others), for which Beckford claimed to have written an air.

C. B. Farinelli (1705–82), King Philip V of Spain's Neapolitan *castrato*, whom Beckford visited in 1781.

response to music. He is suspicious of the frequent emotional phrases in Beckford's descriptions of musical performances, like 'soft voluptuous cadences', and 'plaintive airs'. Of Pacchierotti's singing Beckford wrote:

I start, grow restless, stride about and begin to form ambitious projects. Musick raises before me a host of phantoms which I pursue with eagerness. My blood thrills in my veins, its whole current is changed and agitated. I can no longer command myself, and whilst the phrenzy lasts would willingly be devoted to destruction.

He wrote to Lady Hamilton in a similar vein, 'Alas, it is very true Musick destroys me – and what is worse, I love being destroyed.' These are the words of someone who may genuinely love music, but whose response to it is simply sensuous and uncerebral. The masochistic titillations Beckford derived from listening to performances do not induce the belief that his own singing and playing of the harpsichord were more than mediocre.

Catherine Hamilton became his Egeria. He confessed to her everything about himself in his uninhibited manner. She roundly condemned what she termed his criminal infatuations, and exhorted him to reform. When they parted he promised that he would in future avoid all 'frightful phantoms'. He wrote to her, 'I shall never be . . . good for anything in this world, but composing airs, building towers, forming gardens, collecting old Japan, and writing a journey to China or the moon.' In general terms how right he was, though we in retrospect can credit him with even wider diversity of talent.

What was William Beckford like at the age of twenty? Undoubtedly he was an attractive young man. He was on the small side, slender, well proportioned we are told, which is not however borne out by his portrait by Romney the following year. There the hips, unusually broad, like a woman's, give him a slightly epicene appearance. But whether Romney's figure was a likeness we cannot be sure. His face in youth was certainly handsome, though the nose was rather long. The expression was mischievous when not downright arrogant. His sneer could be daunting The eyes were small, steel grey, of wonderful acuteness. He had a rapid enunciation and when angry the voice rose to a high scream. He had an affected manner, especially when singing. The wit George Selwyn remarked that his singing voice was like a eunuch's, whether natural or feigned he could not tell. His conversation was brilliant, but he could become boring in the pursuit of a well worn subject. He was given to mimicry. He had a habit when silent or concentrating of putting a freckled hand over his mouth. The best portrait of him was probably Hoppner's taken in middle age. The head is still very handsome and the expression highly intelligent, melancholy and reserved. With the approach of old age Beckford's face became beaky, the nose sharp, chin pointed and, as he lost his teeth, the lips drawn in.

The spring and summer of 1781 were spent by Beckford either in

William Beckford, aged twenty-one, by George Romney, now the property of the National Trust, Bearsted Collection, Upton House, Warwicks.

23

Jacques P. de Loutherbourg (1740–1812), painter of battle scenes and designer of theatrical effects at Drury Lane and Fonthill.

London being lionized by the dowagers as an eligible young millionaire, or at Fonthill, playing the harpsichord, collating his diaries and letters from Italy, preparing for his coming-of-age celebrations, philandering with Louisa, writing long confidential letters to her and Lady Hamilton, and complaining even in those golden days of English 'phlegm and frostiness'. Louisa accepted the fact that 'Kitty' Courtenay held the first place in her lover's affections. 'How my heart bounds with transport when I fancy that after Kitty I am the being you prefer to all others!' She took upon herself the role of go-between when the boy was at Powderham for the holidays. During term time at Westminster School Courtenay somehow managed to spend Saturdays and Sundays with his friend in the Begum's Wimpole Street house. Beckford commissioned Romney to paint his portrait as well as his own.

On 29th September the birthday celebrations took place at Splendens on the most extravagant scale. The house party included the Peter Beckfords, old Cozens, Burton, Pacchierotti, Rauzzini the singer and composer of opera, Tenducci the male soprano, both resident in England, and Lady Margaret Gordon (afterwards Beckford's wife), in addition to a horde of relations. A little pastoral cantata, *Il Tributo*, was composed by Rauzzini for the occasion; and for three days Beckford religiously carried out his duties to family, neighbours and tenants with the customary feasting, dancing, bonfires and fireworks. These obligatory festivities were followed at Christmas by another party much more to Beckford's taste. He was at last his own master, he could invite whom he liked.

Again the three Italian musicians were present. So too were Cozens, Louisa (without her husband), her brother George Pitt, her intimate friend Sophia Musters, Beckford's cousins Alexander (afterwards his son-in-law) and Archibald Hamilton, and Kitty Courtenay. Jacques Philippe de Loutherbourg, who had revolutionized theatrical lighting at Drury Lane, experimented with an elaborate invention called the Eidophusikon, a combination of moving pictures accompanied by music, artificial thunder and lightning. The Rev. Samuel Henley, tutor to the Hamilton boys, and an enthusiastic orientalist, contributed to the *Arabian Nights* atmosphere. For several days and nights on end the exclusive party indulged in an orgy of acting, music and love-making. The occasion caused a good deal of scandal in the county (Pitt was conducting a violent affair with Mrs. Musters) and was a landmark in Beckford's life. He looked back upon it as a time of supreme, unalloyed romance, and the germination of his novel *Vathek*. Before the party was over Beckford had handed to Henley for his opinion the Italian letters which were to be printed in 1783 as part of *Dreams, Waking Thoughts and Incidents*.

2 · TARNISHED YOUTH

AMUEL Henley was an archaeologist and writer of some distinction. He was also a seasoned traveller, having spent his early years in America. These attributes, as well as a taste for the exotic and a sinister avuncular manner, attracted Beckford. Here was an older man of letters, an usher at Harrow School, ready to advise a younger genius on the threshold of imaginative authorship. Henley's spontaneous admiration of the Italian letters encouraged Beckford to launch upon the literary work which was to win him lasting fame.

In January 1782 Beckford began writing *Vathek*. 'The fit I laboured under', to quote his own words scribbled in a book, 'lasted two days and a night' without intermission. He wrote in French, for that language came to him as readily as his own. The novel was not completed until the following July, when he handed it to Henley for translation into English.

There is no reason for supposing that *Vathek* was prompted by Henley, but there is reason for assuming that Henley encouraged the undertaking. Beckford announced towards the end of his life that *Vathek* had been inspired by the scenes enacted during the coming-of-age and Christmas parties of 1781 in the Egyptian Hall and vaulted passages at Splendens, peopled as they were by the prototypes of Carathis (Mrs. Beckford), Nourinhar (Louisa), Gulchenrouz (Courtenay) and various female servants. The mysterious glow from rockets, fires and lanterns, the voluptuous twilight cast by the silken hangings and reflecting mirrors of the Turkish Room and the scented smoke from aloe wood burning in gilded cassolettes conjured up the background scenes. Although certain descriptive passages were suggested to the author by a mass of oriental literature and engravings, such as Le Brun's *Voyage par la Moscavie en Perse et aux Indes Orientales*, Jean Chardin's *Voyage en Perse*, Lady Mary Wortley Montagu's *Letters from Turkey*, and even *The Arabian Nights*, to name only some of the source books in which Beckford was well versed (unlike previous writers of eastern romances including Dr Johnson, the author of *Rasselas*), the theme of *Vathek* was wholly the invention of his brain. Moreover it is written in a dead pan prose, bristling with a wicked humour, which entirely redeems the conventional setting and makes the follies and inconsistencies of the story vastly entertaining. It is easy to guess that the book was composed with the minimum forethought and planning. In the middle the humour slackens. Beckford could not keep it up. *Vathek* ends with the serious cautionary moral that unmitigated evil finds its inevitable reward in eternal damnation. Not perhaps to our jaded consciences a novel or even awesome sequel. But to the eighteenth century it was a classic sequel. *Vathek* was warmly commended for 'the

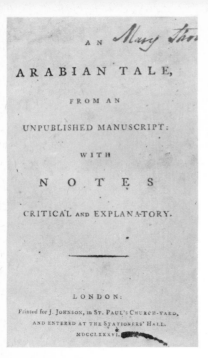

Title page *Vathek* (1786) of Samuel Henley's English edition.

A title page to the French text of *Vathek* (1815). There is almost undue emphasis on the Caliph's visionary powers.

morality of [its] design' and its sublimity by an anonymous reviewer in the *Gentleman's Magazine* (July 1786) who appreciated 'the vivid and elegant descriptions' throughout. A later and more perspicacious reviewer (J. G. Lockhart in the *Quarterly Review*, vol. 51. 1834) found it 'stained with some poison spots . . . We do not allude so much to its audacious licentiousness, as to the diabolical levity of its contempt for mankind.' As André Parreaux has intimated, *Vathek* just had to be written because it was there, waiting like some other of the world's great allegories – *Don Quixote, Pilgrim's Progress*, and *Faust* – to be conjured out of the human mind at a predestined moment.

Henley's part in its production was shabby. At a time when Beckford was abroad in great distress he published an English translation without the author's consent. In a preface he claimed that the tale was translated from an Arabian manuscript, thus covertly intimating to the reader that it was his own composition. His subsequent lame excuse was that Beckford's endless tinkering with the text had driven him distracted, and he could delay publication no longer. Beckford was obliged in 1787 to issue a French re-translation in Lausanne, correcting Henley's misleading assumption and putting forward his just claim to authorship.

Vathek's eventual popularity and influence upon writers was immense. It was followed by numerous picaresque tales with an oriental setting. Byron acknowledged his indebtedness to it in a footnote to the Turkish narrative poem *The Giaour*: 'For correctness of costume, beauty of description, and power of imagination, it far surpasses all European imitations . . . As an Eastern tale, even *Rasselas* must bow before it.' *Anastasius,* a long, tedious novel by Thomas Hope, published in 1819, was likewise set in the oriental scene in which the unscrupulous eponym indulged in a series of discreditable adventures. The young Disraeli's autobiographical romance, *Contarini Fleming*, was certainly inspired by *Vathek* and even submitted to Beckford for comments. The elevation of man's sinfulness to heroic proportions, surpassing Milton's aggrandizement of Satan in *Paradise Lost*, made an appeal to the age of the Picturesque which Samuel Johnson when composing *Rasselas* had never envisaged.

The spring and summer of 1782 which saw the compilation of *Vathek* abounded in social distractions. One of these was the production in London of a pastoral operetta, for which Lady Craven wrote the libretto and Beckford the music, and in which the stars Bertoni, Barthélémon, Pacchierotti and Burton were performers. The composer acknowledged that his contribution was mediocre.

The affair with Louisa, meanwhile, was causing embarrassment within the family and chatter outside it. This time it was Louisa who threw discretion to the winds. She did not care who knew about her passion for her first cousin by marriage. She had grown to loathe her luckless husband, even considering how she could murder him. Added to the knowledge that she played second fiddle to Kitty, rumours now reached her of the probable engagement of her idol to Lady Margaret Gordon. 'Why must she possess lawfully and eternally what I would suffer ten thousand deaths to enjoy one instant? William, it must not be,' she wrote in desperation. William's reaction was to clear out.

In May he left England with an impressive entourage – his chaplain, our old friend the Rev. John Lettice in another role, his musician John Burton, and painter J. R. Cozens, the gifted son of Alexander. The grand equipage of three carriages and outriders was in Austria mistaken for that of the Emperor travelling incognito, and charged accordingly at the several inns it halted at. In Venice Beckford was reunited with some of his old raffish friends who accompanied him to Padua where he paid his respects at the shrine of his favourite Saint Antony. In Rome he actually received a short note from Courtenay, to which he replied with ecstasy,

I read your letter with a beating heart, my dearest Willy, and kissed it a thousand times. It is needless for me to repeat that I am miserable without you. You know I can scarcely be said to live in your absence.

In Rome, too, he wrote the concluding letter of *Dreams, Waking Thoughts and Incidents*.

When he reached the ultimate goal, Naples, in July, his burning enthusiasms momentarily turned to ashes. His beloved Lady Hamilton was dying, and Sir William was desolate. Then poor Burton was suddenly stricken with fever and died, 'execrating in the most shocking manner the person who was incidentally instrumental, as he thought, in bringing him into this deplorable situation', according to the artist Thomas Jones. 'Little Cousins', in spite of his proficiency with Handel on the violin, appears not to have given entire satisfaction and the association soon came to an end, not however without his having produced nearly a hundred landscape scenes remarkable for their tranquil tones of blue and green. Beckford in later years referred to J. R. Cozens as an ungrateful scoundrel, and when the artist went mad, declined to assist him financially.

Beckford was home again in November to be greeted with the news that Louisa was dying. The wretched woman, riddled with tuberculosis, implored him to come to her. As far as we know, he never did. Beckford was one of those people who could not face up to scenes, recriminations or the sufferings of others. Instead, by steeling himself against sentiment he prevented all claims of affection from reaching his heart. Louisa was undoubtedly silly, and hysterical, but her unrequited love letters to Beckford are among the most tragic in the English language.

By March 1783 troubles were brewing for Beckford. *Dreams, Waking Thoughts* was printed, and suddenly withdrawn on pressure from the family. It is difficult to understand what were the relations' objections to these seemingly innocuous travel letters. It may have been that they were ostensibly addressed to Louisa, that their tone was frivolous, that their tenor was pro-Catholic yet mocking of Christian dogma, and that they

Elizabeth Lady Craven, later Margravine of Anspach, with whom Beckford wrote an operetta in 1782.

27

were too subjective to be respectable; that they were too soppy about animals and too anti-blood sport; that they were in short effeminate and altogether un-English. The Begum doubtless found references to 'perfumed apartments', the reading of Spenser's poetry in alcoves, and accounts of her son bounding like an antelope in ecstasies or flitting 'childishly like a butterfly in a parterre' not the sort of self-portraiture likely to appeal to the constituents of Hindon's rotten borough. At all events the withdrawal of *Dreams, Waking Thoughts* from publication was another literary reverse for Beckford. The letters, admittedly, do not amount to his best writing: although they contain some fine descriptive passages, they are a little too facetious, a little too precious.

On 29th March Beckford wrote a letter to Louisa, then in France for her health, confirming his undying love for Courtenay, who appended a postscript telling her that they were together, having 'lived so long in Hell. You cannot imagine how much we have been persecuted.' This persecution came from Kitty's suspicious father and aunt Charlotte, who having failed to elicit any return of affection from Beckford, had the previous September married the one man in England best equipped by his inclination and position to cause Beckford irreparable harm. Alexander Wedderburn, now Lord Chief Justice of the Court of Common Pleas and Baron Loughborough, was arguably the most treacherous and bigoted low churchman ever to have presided over the British bench of judges. He had been stung by the undisguised criticism and mockery of the young man whose father, the Whig Alderman, had been a detested political enemy. The Loughboroughs united to vent their righteous indignation and vengeance upon the millionaire playboy, as they saw him, who had cynically corrupted the innocent heir to the ancient Courtenay title.

On 5th May Beckford was married to Lady Margaret Gordon, the pretty and charming twenty-year-old daughter of the 4th Earl of Aboyne. The couple immediately went to Switzerland for their honeymoon. Louisa was distraught, Kitty Courtenay was as much loved as ever, and Lady Margaret treated by her ambivalent husband with solicitude and kindness, which turned to deep devotion. For her part Lady Margaret was in love with Beckford and when disaster befell him never wavered in her loyalty and defence. Throughout her short life she behaved with such exemplary goodness that Beckford worshipped her memory throughout the fifty-eight years of his widowerhood.

Nevertheless Beckford was during the honeymoon, to put it mildly, in an emotional tangle. He wrote from Sécheron to his old confidant Alexander Cozens, 'Innumerable fancies rush upon me. Strange hopes and as strange fears! During these moments I dream of Wm and of Fonthill whilst the confused murmur of leaves and water lulls me to sound rest. Lady M walks about gathering flowers from the Shrubs which almost dip their boughs in the Lake. Why am I not happy? – Is it not my own fault that I am miserable?' Comment seems superfluous.

Alexander Wedderburn, created Lord Loughborough and 1st Earl of Rosslyn in 1801. He married the Hon. Charlotte Courtenay and threatened to prosecute Beckford in 1784. Portrait by W. Owen.

In March 1784 the married couple were installed in Splendens. Beckford wrote to Cozens, who was alive to every oblique innuendo of his correspondent, to 'assure you I am as Indian as ever. With respect to Wm I have been for this fortnight past in total darkness. How I long for the sight of his lovely countenance.' The Beckfords were presented at court. The twenty-three-year-old husband procured his parliamentary election for Wells, long held by his Hamilton relations, and was already jockeying for a peerage. The Begum was all smiles over the apparent fulfilment of her ambitions. Louisa was now quite out of the running, and as for young Courtenay the dark shadow seemed to be lifting under the sunshine radiating from Lady Margaret's adoring eyes. To Henley settled in a Suffolk rectory, to whose custody Beckford had been intriguing for Kitty to be entrusted, he wrote that this young man was 'quite lost in flowers and foolery at present . . . [his] character, I fear, still more girlish and trifling than you are aware of.' The scales were already beginning to fall.

Lady Margaret Beckford (née Gordon), Beckford's wife, who died in 1786. From a miniature by Maria Cosway.

With June came a tragic turn in Beckford's fortunes. Lady Margaret gave birth to a still-born son. Lord Courtenay, now intensely on the alert, refused to send Kitty to Henley. In October Beckford's name was gazetted among others about to be made peers. The title of Lord Beckford of Fonthill was actually inscribed on the patent. Both Beckfords were staying at Powderham. Ill-omened visit. The Loughboroughs were staying there too. Within a fortnight Beckford was discovered very early one morning in Kitty's bedroom by the boy's tutor. This gentleman heard 'a creeking and bustle, which raised his curiosity, & thro' the key hole he saw the operation, which it seems he did not interrupt, but informed Lord C, & the whole was blown up,' Charles Greville wrote to Sir William Hamilton. Beckford was accused by Loughborough and resolutely refused to admit culpability. He had, he asseverated, been thrashing Courtenay. Kitty however was forced to confess and surrender letters. Sodomy was at the time a capital offence. By November the newspapers had resorted to every indecent allegation. *The Morning Herald* of 27th declared piously, 'The rumour concerning a Grammatical mistake of Mr. B. and the Hon. Mr. C. in regard to the genders, we hope for the honour of Nature originates in Calumny!' Other newspapers were less equivocal. A conclave of Beckfords, Gordons and Courtenays met to express horror and advice. The Mayfair blue-stockings were agog. They had of course foreseen disaster and disgrace all along. Miss Elizabeth Carter wrote to Mrs. Montagu that 'when he . . . so extravagantly and ridiculously addicted himself to music, all prospect of his becoming great or respectable was over'. It was as simple as that. Only the Begum and Lady Margaret kept their heads and staunchly maintained Beckford's innocence. Mrs. Beckford made the sensible suggestion that her son should pick up half a dozen harlots in Covent Garden and parade them in Mayfair. Lady Margaret counselled flight. Unfortunately she could not accompany him because she was again pregnant. On 29th October Beckford set forth, but

29

Beckford's daughters, Margaret (afterwards Mrs. Orde) and Susan (afterwards Duchess of Hamilton), when children. Portrait by George Romney.

at Dover his self-pride and courage overcame his apprehensions and he returned to Fonthill.

The long and the short of this distressing business was twofold. No prosecution took place, which points to the fact that the totally unscrupulous Loughborough could rake up no proof of crime having been committed. But Beckford's good name was gone. He was ostracized from English society and subjected to snubs and hostility for the remaining sixty years of his life. His character in consequence was gravely affected. A naturally high-strung, acutely sensitive man with few illusions about the nature of his fellow beings, he grew increasingly embittered, ruthless and cruel. He became solitary, introspective and – let us recognize it – more and more deeply immersed in his multivarious intellectual and artistic interests.

The break with Kitty was complete. Henceforth Beckford barely suffered his name to pass his lips. In the Portuguese Journal of 1787 he reviled him for allowing 'the most obnoxious papers [how incriminating were they?] to remain in old Beelzebub [Loughborough's] clutches', and called him 'that cowardly effeminate fool, Wm Courtenay'. Indeed Courtenay's character and conduct deteriorated with age. In 1811 he was forced to flee the country to avoid facing a charge of sodomy, and never returned. In 1785 the Beckfords retired to Switzerland where the following year Lady Margaret, after giving birth to a second daughter, died of puerperal fever.

Beckford was heartbroken. The one being who not only remained loyal but refrained from censure, whose gentle innocence was so unaffected that he, hardened cynic, far from mocking, revered it; and who, had she lived, might have softened the harsh edges of his abrasive temper, had left him for ever. Furthermore, she had left him with two babies with whom he had not the least idea what to do. He immediately packed them off to London for the Begum to look after. In his tribulation he had the chagrin of reading reports in the British press that his flagitious behaviour had been responsible for his wife's death. His English friends ceased to correspond. Henley pirated the literary work by which he set greatest store. Thus injured he alternately mourned his wretched fate and railed against his countrymen.

However even the crushing bereavement and Henley's treachery could not subdue his natural high spirits for more than a few months. Buoyed up by the sympathy shown him by his Swiss friends – the residents of Vevey presented him with a memorial protesting against the vile insinuations of his countrymen – Beckford, as already mentioned, re-issued Vathek, and resumed the prolonged process begun at Fonthill immediately after the Powderham scandal, of titivating and falsifying his old letters with a view to their ultimate publication.

3 · PORTUGUESE SUMMER

I N January 1787 Beckford slunk back to Fonthill where he was joined by his half-sister Elizabeth Harvey, the Begum's daughter by her first husband. He had no intention of remaining in England to afford his county neighbours the satisfaction of cutting him. So having attended to affairs he went abroad in March with a large train of servants. Also in attendance were the Swiss physician François Verdeil, who had helped him with the re-translation of *Vathek*, and his erstwhile tutor the prudish Robert Drysdale. On his engagement the previous November Drysdale had written to a friend, 'There is something very disagreeable in his history – but I am certain he means to behave well or he would not have chosen me for a Companion . . .' which is very probable. Drysdale was to remain with Beckford until 1790.

On leaving Fonthill Beckford's intention was to visit his Jamaican properties. Had he ever got there he might well, with his natural sympathy for the underdog, have improved the lot of his multitude of slaves. But when he reached Falmouth and boarded the hired ship, which was swarming with cockroaches, the prospect of crossing the Atlantic in winter gales with such company daunted him. Instead he sailed to Madeira and on to Lisbon.

There now ensued a year and a half of Beckford's long life which gave rise to what, in my opinion, is far and away the best thing he ever wrote, *The Journal in Portugal and Spain 1787–1788*. This is the original manuscript out of which Beckford in old age fashioned the bogus letters (addressed to nobody in particular) of *Italy, with Sketches of Spain and Portugal*, vol. II. Mr. Boyd Alexander discovered the *Journal* among the Hamilton Papers and published it unaltered in 1954. The *Journal* is written in a free and absolutely uninhibited prose. It includes what the bowdlerized version omits, namely Beckford's amatory adventures and his nagging desire to be accepted by the Portuguese court. In its racy fashion the *Journal* conveys an unrivalled picture of life in Portuguese royal and patrician circles before the purgative winds of the French Revolution had blown away the perfumes and stinks of ceremonial and misery from a land governed by the Church, which provided the populace with not merely rules of conduct but the greater part of its pageantry and fun. Beckford's descriptions conjure up a kind of *Alice in Wonderland* world, in which nothing is unexpected, where marquises and dwarfs, mitred abbots and peasants dance an eternal fandango of high spirits and silliness.

When the ship with Beckford's party aboard first entered the mouth of the Tagus the Custom House guards made the captain sign on behalf of himself, crew and passengers a set of articles containing such phrases as these:

that they will take off their hats to the clergy . . . that they will kneel at the Elevation of the Host; that they will in no way insult the Cross, wherever set up, by making water, but however urgent their Necessities may be, will retain the same till a proper and lawful distance.

This was the prologue to a succession of incidents no less fantastical. Beckford lost no time in renting the Quinta dos Bichos, close to the Palaçio das Necessidades, the royal residence on the outskirts of Lisbon on the road to Belem. Within a short time he had become acquainted with the Marialvas, a leading aristocratic family in Portugal and Hereditary Masters of the Horse, of whom Diogo, afterwards 5th Marquis of Marialva, was in daily contact with the reigning Queen Maria I. Charmed by the young millionaire widower, who was so markedly different from the usual insolent Englishman, Diogo took an inordinate fancy to him and introduced him to his entire family. Beckford's wit, ability to speak several languages, erudition, love of music and curiosity to learn all there was to know of Portuguese art and history enchanted the exclusive Marialva family who were insular, old-fashioned, unlearned and religiously credulous to a degree that their new friend found almost unbelievable and very endearing. He of course played up to them shamelessly by assuming a devoutness which for a heretic amazed as much as it pleased them. 'The Marquis', as Beckford always referred to Diogo, (whose father known as 'the old Marquis', was still alive), regarded him like a son – he hoped indeed to marry him to his daughter – and did everything in his power to make him renounce England for good and live permanently in Portugal. Try as the Marquis did, nothing would induce the English Minister, Robert Walpole, to present his *déclassé* countryman to the Queen. And through no other channel could an introduction to the Portuguese court be brought about. Marialva's endeavours and Beckford's frustrations on this score run like a theme through the *Journal*, interwoven with the author's amused, irritated and often bored reactions to his host's affection for him, and his descriptions of Portuguese customs, religious observances and landscape, which are unfailingly, sharp and comical.

Here, for example, is Beckford's vignette of a room in a Portuguese nobleman's house:

No glasses, no pictures, no gilding, no decoration but heavy drapery; even the tables are concealed by cut velvet flounces, in the style of those with which our dowagers used formerly to array their toilets. The very sight of such close tables is enough to make one perspire, and I cannot imagine what demon prompted the Portuguese to invent such a fusty fashion, hideous everywhere, but particularly so in a climate as sultry as their own.

And here an allusion to the old Marquis of Marialva's gluttony – he was seventy-four:

I can hardly credit what he [the Abbade, the family confessor] told me of the old Marquis, my friend's father's voracity, of his eating two dozen partridges, a whole ham at a meal. According to the Abbade thirty-five dishes the most exquisite that can be procured, beside the dessert, are served up every day to this prince of gluttons, who always dines alone between two tubs ready to receive what he has no longer room to contain and remains three hours at table.

Practically every day the Marquis dined with Beckford or Beckford dined with the Marquis. The Marialva children adored the strange foreigner, regarding him as a sort of elder brother. Beckford returned their affection, and in the case of the thirteen-year old son, Dom Pedro, rather more warmly than Dr. Verdeil thought suitable. After a drunken dinner party at which Beckford embraced Dom Pedro ('I have tasted the sweetness of his lips. His dear eyes have confessed the secret of his bosom') the alarmed doctor counselled their leaving Portugal before the young heir betrayed his attachment. Fortunately the affair petered out and the doctor's forebodings were not realized. Beckford maintained in the Marialva family his reputation for sanctity until the end of his sojourn. Sunday after Sunday and saint's day after saint's day he attended masses with the Marquis. On 4th November they worshipped at the convent of the Boa Morte.

I shook all over with piety, and so did the Marquis, and my knees are become horny with frequent kneelings. Verdeil thinks I shall end in a hermitage or go mad – perhaps both; he says, too, I have rendered the Marquis ten times more fervent than before and that by mutually encouraging each other we shall soon produce fruits worthy of Bedlam. To be sure I have a devout turn and a pretty manner of thumping myself, but there are twenty or thirty thousand good souls who thump better than me. This morning at Boa Morte one shrivelled sinner remained, the whole time our Mass lasted, with outstretched arms in the attitude and with the inflexible stiffness of an old-fashioned candlestick. Another contrite personage was so affected at the moment of consecration that he flattened his nose on the ground and licked the pavement. When shall I have sufficient grace to be so beastly!

The following day the two friends paid a pious visit to the descendants of the Holy Crows who had torn out the eyes of the murderers of St. Vincent, patron saint of Lisbon Cathedral.

It was late when we entered this gloomy edifice [the cloisters of São Vicente] and the crows, I believe, were gone quietly to roost, but a sacristan, seeing us approach, officiously roused them. Oh, how sleek and plump and glossy they are. My admiration of their size, their plumage and their deep-toned croakings carried me, I fear, beyond the bounds of saintly decorum. I was just stretching forth my hand to stroke their feathers when the Marquis checked me with a solemn forbidding look. D. Pedro and the Grand Prior, aware of the proper ceremonial, kept a respectful distance, whilst the sacristan and an old toothless priest, almost bent double, communicated a long string of anecdotes concerning these present Holy Crows, their immediate predecessors, and other crows in the old time before them. The Marquis listened with implicit faith and attention, never opened his lips during the half hour we remained, except to enforce our veneration and to exclaim with the most pious composure, *Honorado Corvo*.

33

A more profane diversion was making and listening to music either in the Quinta dos Bichos or, when the weather in Lisbon became intolerably hot, at the Quinta da Ramalhão which Beckford had rented near Cintra so as to be next door to the Marialvas' summer resort. Here in the dining room, with walls deliciously frescoed by Jean Pillement so as to resemble an arbour alive with painted birds and flowers, Jeronimo da Lima, conductor of the Royal Opera House, would assemble round the central grotto table a group of musicians to play and sing his compositions for opera and oratorio. The memory of these carefree summer evenings were a never-failing delight to Beckford in the years to come. All the while the Marquis, who was not the least musical, would sit staring out of the window, tapping with his foot or humming out of tune. When Beckford could bear the distraction no longer he would clear the floor, dance minuets with Dom Pedro, run hand in hand with him down the garden alleys, or allow the Marquis, whose pleasures were simple, to hold a handkerchief four feet from the floor for Beckford to leap over.

At the patriarchal church in Lisbon Beckford would during the interminable sermons steal up to the musicians' gallery and watch and listen to Polycarpo da Silva, first tenor of the Queen's Chapel, playing the harpsichord. Polycarpo easily persuaded him to hear one of his most talented pupils at the seminary give a rendering of Haydn on this instrument. And so came about the introduction to Gregorio Franchi, the seventeen-year-old son of an Italian singer at court. Beckford was entranced with both the playing and the player. The very prospect of the meeting had occasioned the remark, 'I shall get into a scrape if I don't take care. How tired I am of keeping a Mask on my face. How tight it sticks – it makes me sore.' The meeting led to clandestine visits by Franchi to the Quinta dos Bichos where he and Beckford played sonatas and sang together by the hour. There are frequent references in the *Journal*, such as the following, 'Franchi came sneaking in at tea time. I felt confused and guilty', and 'At tea time Franchi came in and we played like kittens.' They were joined by the Marquis, and all danced entrechats. Soon Franchi entered Beckford's service as accompanist, followed him to Madrid and remained in his service for forty years. An accomplished singer and pianist he was furthermore an outstandingly sweet character. The presence at Fonthill of the 'Portugal orange' as the Wiltshire neighbours called the faithful Franchi, was the cause of unmerited gossip and tales of unmentionable goings-on at the Abbey, which were wholly fictitious. During one of Beckford's subsequent visits to Portugal Franchi was at Marialva's instigation made a Chevalier of the Order of Christ.

By the end of 1787 there were no signs of the obdurate Walpole relenting. There were no invitations to those court functions which the least distinguished English residents in Portugal automatically acquired. Hurt and piqued, Beckford decided to leave. The Marialvas were in despair. In December Beckford packed his luggage and set off for Spain.

In Madrid he was received by an old friend whom he had known in Paris, the Dowager Duchess of Berwick, a sister of Princess Louise of Stolberg, the estranged wife of Prince Charles Stuart and mistress of the Italian poet Count Alfieri. The Duchess, being extremely musical, gave parties at which Beckford met the best musicians in Spain and himself participated in drawing-room concerts. Madrid society lacked the old-fashioned insularity of the Lisbon aristocracy, was more cosmopolitan and more formal; and its demands upon Beckford's company were more exacting. He had not been in the capital more than two days before a certain Chevalier de Rojas called at his lodgings and offered his services as cicerone. This man, who knew everyone in Madrid who was anyone, was the acknowledged 'obedient humble servant and cortejo' of one of Madrid's leading society ladies, the Countess of Aranda. Into her house Beckford was immediately precipitated. He described it as 'half-Spanish, half-French, [with] small glasses in heavy frames, fuming braziers that made my head swim. I was plagued too with gripes in the gizzard.' Madame de Aranda was married to her uncle, 'old enough to be her grandfather, [and] looks as sickly and drooping as a narcissus or lily of the valley would appear if stuck in Abraham's bosom and continually breathed upon by that venerable patriarch.'

The twenty-seven-year-old Englishman was courted and fêted without cessation. Once again he became hopelessly entangled in webs of amorous intrigue. He was enamoured of the French Ambassador's eighteen-year-old daughter, the Princesse de Listenais, and her fourteen-year-old husband, and her brother, the nineteen-year-old Prince de Carency, all at the same time. He was the recipient of passionate love letters from the Marquess of Santa Cruz's wife who expressed wild jealousy of a choir boy, 'ce maudit petit Ki-Ki', and he carried out a mild flirtation with the Tripolitan Ambassador's brother, a Mussulman youth of twelve.

It is hardly surprising that before six months were up Beckford was worn out. Besides, trouble was looming again. The French Ambassador forbade his daughter to see her dangerous admirer, but whether he put a similar embargo upon his son and son-in-law we do not know. Moreover Beckford came against the same obstacle in Madrid as he had encountered in Lisbon: the British chargé d'affaires refused to present him at court. In June 1788 Beckford wisely took refuge in flight to Paris.

Towards the end of the year the death of Lord Courtenay and Kitty's succession to the title made Beckford's return to England less likely to be followed by prosecution or harassment.

In October 1789 he was back at Fonthill inspecting the redecoration and refurnishing of Splendens which in his absence had been put in the hands of Messrs. Foxhall & Fryer of Old Cavendish Street. He also inspected some new chimneypieces carved by the sculptors Bacon and Banks, and two capital views of Wales which Loutherbourg had painted for the Great Apartment. During this visit his sole companions were

Rutter's view of the scenery of the American Plantation, immediately to the east of Bitham Lake.

Franchi and a Spanish dwarf. No neighbours called. His children were in the care of his mother in London under the tuition of Lettice.

The next few years were restless ones, spent between England and Paris. During his absences abroad he directed by correspondence the afforestation and landscaping of Fonthill on a vast scale. Larch, spruce and fir were planted on the barren hills to screen his domain from the curious, and a twenty-mile road was planned to meander through the grounds. Robert Drysdale rejoined him at Fonthill in June of 1791. There were, the tutor wrote, three chefs and one confectioner employed in the kitchen, and ten footmen waiting at table upon three persons. Yet his host slept upon a narrow truckle bed like a child's. His habits were in most respects ascetic. He rose each morning at six, breakfasted at ten and dined at half past three. He ate and drank sparingly and rode his horse every day round the estate.

He paid two long visits to Paris during the Revolution when the French upper classes were being systematically guillotined and even rich foreigners thought fit to leave the country. Beckford by contrast was never so well off as at this particular moment. His annual income, according to Farington, was now £155,000. He accordingly took every advantage of the prevailing conditions in Paris by buying dirt cheap precious furniture and rare books then being dispersed from private hands and the royal *garde-meuble*.

Since his earliest years Beckford was attracted by rococo porcelain and furniture. He fell in love with and bought the Meissen dinner service of 363 pieces made specially for the Stadholder William V and painted with views of Dutch ports and cities. He liked Buhl furniture, or rather to quote his own words, 'I adore the true, capital buhl, but it must be the best.' Of such were a pair of *armoires* from the Louvre palace which he bought. It is

36

hardly surprising that a man of his refinement admired the furniture which the French *ébénistes* were producing just before and during his youth – the most exquisite artifacts which the civilized world has yet seen; and that he should laud to the skies Madame de Pompadour as the greatest connoisseur who ever lived. He had the satisfaction of acquiring the outstanding 'Van Dieman' black lacquer box (c. 1635–45), decorated in gold and silver with scenes of Japanese court life, which had belonged to her. As though in acknowledgement of her unchallenged status as leading patron of the Louis Quinze style, he bought during the Revolution (and it is typical of him to have been completely indifferent to the fact that it was then out of date) the roll-top desk made in 1769 by J. H. Riesener, known as *Le Bureau du Roi Stanislaus* (of Poland), which is now in the Wallace Collection. In 1792 he had furniture specially made in Paris under the direction of the royal goldsmith, R. J. Auguste, 'in the true spirit of Corinth and Athens'.

In his old age Beckford declared that on the outbreak of the French Revolution 'he felt all the enthusiasms of the time in favour of liberty, enthusiasms quickly checked by subsequent events.' After the execution of King Louis XVI in January 1793 France declared war on England; and Beckford was an enemy alien, as it were behind the lines. His life was in danger. But his faithful bookseller Chardin helped him to work, disguised as an assistant, in the famous Mérigot's bookshop.

He returned to Portugal at least twice. The second visit was in November 1793. The old magic had not entirely evaporated, but things were not quite the same as they had been. In the first place he was older. In the second, the peninsula had been a little shaken by events in France. Nevertheless the kind Marialvas welcomed him with open arms in spite of the fact that he had not married the Marquis's daughter Henriqueta. All the old Portuguese friends rallied and the prodigal resumed his religious

The 'Van Dieman' black lacquer box (c. 1635–45) which once belonged to Madame de Pompadour. Now in the Victoria and Albert Museum.

Le Bureau du Roi Stanislaus (of Poland) by J. H. Riesener, 1769, acquired by Beckford during the French Revolution.

exercises, in particular his attention to St. Antony. He built himself a house at the mouth of the Tagus, of which a surviving plan in his own hand, dated December 1793, has been shown by Mr. Boyd Alexander to foreshadow the enfilade of apartments at Fonthill Abbey. He also rented a house at Cintra, called Monserrate, which had been built by an English merchant in 1790. Here he laid out the loveliest *quinta* in the whole of Portugal. This visit achieved two things: Beckford's belated presentation at the Portuguese court, although not to poor Queen Maria I (by now hopelessly insane), but to her son the Regent Prince of Brazil; and the famous excursion to the monasteries of Alcobaça and Batalha, accompanied by the nonagenarian Prior of Aviz, Franchi and Dr. Ehrhart, his Alsatian physician. The fruits of the excursion were to be garnered over forty years later from notes taken at the time. *The Recollections*, published in 1835, are the culminating tribute of the old Beckford to some of the happiest days of his youth in a society not completely overturned by the consequences of the French Revolution. How often, he then wrote, had he not blessed 'the hour when my steps were directed to Portugal! As I sat in the nook of my retired window' of an ancient mansion on the road to

38

Batalha, 'I looked with complacency on a roof which sheltered no scheming hypocrites – on tables, on which perhaps no newspaper had ever been thrown, and on neat white pillows, guiltless of propping up the heads of those assassins of real prosperity – political adventurers.' That is what his reminiscences of Portugal meant to him. The country was a sort of haven from the horrors of the modern world, at least in his old man's memory.

His *Recollections of an Excursion to the Monasteries of Alcobaça and Batalha*, is, unlike the impromptu, uninhibited *Journal*, a literary *tour de force*. Like the other it presents a galaxy of lively impressions and sketches overflowing with poignancy, mockery, affection and irritation. Yet it lacks a forthright spontaneity. It emits just the faintest whiff of the lamp. Situations are too contrived to be convincingly fortuitous. Descriptions

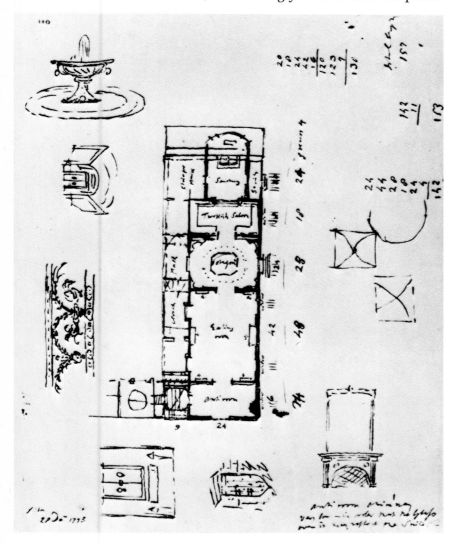

Beckford's plan of his Lisbon house, drawn by himself and showing affinities with the future plan of Fonthill Abbey.

39

are at times too full of superlatives: 'a preparation of the freshest eggs ever laid, with the richest suger ever distilled from the finest canes ever grown in the Brazils . . . under the most skilful management.' Nevertheless what travel writing before or since has been so high-spirited, so poetical, or so entertaining? Who can read without merriment the picture of the three Grand Priors marching hand in hand to the kitchen of Alcobaça to inspect the feast that is about to be served them? Or without wonder the description of the author's arrival at Batalha by moonlight, 'the buttresses and pinnacles, and fretted spires' of the great abbey 'towering in all their pride, and marking the ground with deep shadows that appeared interminable'? Or without emotion the account of the solemn procession through the nave of Batalha church, with the gold and ruby light streaming through the long windows upon the white vestments of the slowly advancing monks? Or without shuddering in horror at 'the most terrible, the most agonizing shrieks' uttered by mad Queen Maria, 'Ai Jesous! Ai Jesous!' which echoed down the corridors of Queluz Palace? Do we not positively smell 'the effluvia, neither of jasmine nor of roses – in short, that species of high conventual frowziness which monastic habits and garments are not a little apt to engender' in hot weather, of the hundred venerable fathers assembled to watch – of all things – a play? And want indignantly to rebut the absurd allegation of the bird queen that England was too cold a country 'to allow [birds], sweet dears to build their nests and enjoy themselves'?

The boathouse beside Fonthill lake.
Vignette in Rutter's *Delineations of Fonthill.*

4 · FONTHILL ABBEY

HE year 1795 saw the end of Beckford's romance with Portugal. He went there again three years later, but it was the perfunctory visit of a disillusioned lover to his neglected mistress. The year 1795 also saw the end of Beckford's youth and the end of his creative writing. The material for all his subsequent writings, such as they were, had already been gathered. The inspiration was harvested, bottled up, awaiting release whenever required. Henceforth Beckford's creative forces were to be directed into other channels. And of course the first of these was building.

Beckford never claimed to be an amateur architect in the sense that, for example, Lord Burlington did. He liked it to be believed that as a child he had been taught the rudiments of architecture by Sir William Chambers. Like many a connoisseur he had in his library a quantity of books on architecture – by Vitruvius, du Cerceau, Piranesi, Chambers indeed, Adam, P. F. Robinson and, at the end of his life, even A. W. Pugin. Many were annotated by him. Yet none of Beckford's descriptions of the great buildings he saw is the least professional. All are literary and not very profound at that. Until he was in his thirties he did not seem particularly drawn to the Gothic style. In 1780 he admired San Giorgio Maggiore in Venice as 'by far the most perfect and beautiful edifice my eyes ever beheld . . . I entered the nave, and applauded the genius of Palladio.' In Florence his keen eyes observed that 'The architect [of the Duomo] seems to have turned his building inside out; nothing in art being more ornamented than the exterior, and few churches so simple within.' He found the city of Lucca ugly and gloomy, and only redeemed by its rural setting. The Pisa duomo was 'far the most curious and highly finished edifice my eyes ever viewed.' He detected in it an oriental flavour. As for the famous polychrome façade of Siena cathedral it was 'ridiculous', and the nave floor resembled a Brussels tapestry with hobgoblin figures. Beckford wasted little time in deciding whether a building pleased him or not. A Bath architect recorded how he requested opinion of a new church he had just finished. Beckford accompanied by his dwarf galloped round it one bright moonlit night without stopping. When he came within seeing distance of the church he merely raised his eyes, put spurs to his horse and galloped away faster than before. No comment was vouchsafed, and the architect pressed for none.

By the 1790s Beckford's taste was veering away from the oriental, although he never lost his addiction to the exotic, and was rejecting the classical as ponderous and dull. It is doubtful whether if asked, he would have still endorsed his praise of Palladio, for he was bored stiff with the

James Wyatt (1746–1813),
architect of Fonthill Abbey.
Bust by J. C. F. Rossi, 1797.

essentially Palladian Splendens. The house no longer gave sufficient scope to his progressively Romantic inclinations. The Gothic happened to be, as Kenneth Clark has pointed out, an opportune means of satisfying his exoticism and sense of drama. Unlike Horace Walpole he was not the least concerned with medieval antiquarianism and the reproduction of correct detail. All he was concerned with was creating theatrical effects. In this respect his Fonthill Abbey should not be classified among eighteenth-century Gothic Revival buildings. Rather it anticipated the nineteenth-century search for a new Gothic style. Once again Beckford was looking forwards rather than backwards.

All his life however he had been obsessed with heights and towers. There is not the least need to read a Freudian significance into this propensity. As a boy of seventeen he described to Cozens the imaginary tower he would build in an escape from 'the land of men' into 'an air uncontaminated with the breath of wretches, the objects of our contempt and detestation.' This was a foretaste of his hero Vathek's motives for raising a tower of 11,000 stairs in order to look down upon 'men not larger than pismires, mountains than shells and cities than beehives.' On his first day in Rome in 1780 he expressed a wish that His Holiness would allow him to erect a little tabernacle on St. Peter's dome whence he might survey the city whenever he felt inclined. In Venice his favourite recreation was to 'run up' to the top of the Campanile with the agility of a squirrel. All his life he was fascinated by paintings which included towers, and possessed one by Valckenborsch of the building of the Tower of Babel.

At first Beckford had no intention of building anything on the enormous scale which the Abbey eventually assumed. In 1790 he was toying with the idea of embellishing the estate with a few romantic ruins, just as hundreds of English landowners were doing all over the country. The following year he summoned James Wyatt, who typically put off coming, and Beckford left for abroad without seeing him. Back in England in 1793 Beckford managed to extract from the architect some vague projects for a modern 'chapel' on Stop Beacon, the highest point of the estate where the Alderman had once started to build a tower. The scheme was not adopted. The meeting when it did take place in 1794 was the beginning of a long love-hate between the two ill-assorted men. Wyatt told Farington that on first seeing Beckford he took him for a picture dealer, and not a gentleman. Beckford told Farington that 'if Wyatt can get near a large fire and have a bottle by him he cares for nothing else.' Certainly Wyatt's indolence and procrastination drove Beckford, who was extremely businesslike and precipitate once he had made up his mind, to impotent fury. In letters to Franchi, Beckford referred to the architect as 'Bagasse' (the usual appellation), meaning whore-monger, 'that infamous swine', 'Don Cloaca', and only occasionally as 'dear, angelic most p-p-p-p-perfect Bagasse'.

It was in 1793 that Beckford came upon a pack of hounds hunting in his grounds. Enraged, he gave orders for a twelve-foot wall of seven miles length (called the Barrier) to be erected round the inner domain within twelve months. It was duly carried out, not quite within the time specified, and provided with a *chevaux de frise* of iron spikes along the top.

In 1796 Beckford returned to Fonthill after the second Portuguese sojourn, more or less for good. He was in a state of great indignation because the political mission entrusted to him by the Regent of Portugal to the British Government had been rebuffed by William Pitt's ministry. Pitt, once his boyhood friend, was like everyone else in England turning up his long nose at the man of tarnished reputation. The effect was to drive Beckford more and more into a state of defiance and bravado. He bought an additional 1,700 acres to augment the Fonthill estate. He planted a million trees. He decided once and for all to raise himself a building of a size, style and magnificence that no one in England had ever seen and, what is more, that only a few people in England should see. He would keep the world at bay. Only a handful of the choicest, most intimate friends, who still acknowledged his position in society, would be welcomed. They unfortunately happened to be people like Elizabeth Lady Craven and Emma Lady Hamilton whose respectability the world barely acknowledged to be less tarnished than his own. In this spirit he called upon Bagasse once more, and commissioned him immediately to draw plans for a conventual building with a gigantic tower attached. 'Some people drink to forget their unhappiness,' he said. 'I do not drink, I build.'

He looked around for other ways in which to avenge himself on mankind. Edward Gibbon, the historian, had insulted him after his wife's death in Switzerland. Gibbon was now dead. His library of 6,000 volumes was for sale. Gibbon had left directions to his executors that his books were not to be kept locked up 'under the key of a jealous master', where the public could not make use of them. Beckford did not particularly want the library but he instructed his Swiss friend Dr. Schöll to buy the lot for him, and then did keep the books locked up, in Lausanne. Once only, in 1801, he went to look at them. Having read himself 'nearly blind' as he put it, for a week, he gave Gibbon's library, as though it were a thing of paltry significance, to Dr. Schöll.

By October 1796 Beckford and Wyatt were hastily running up a mock abbey at the far end of the ridge, called Hinkley Hill, from Stop Beacon. The site was less constricted and more accessible than Stop Beacon. Hundreds of workmen were being employed. At Christmas Beckford ostentatiously gave a gargantuan feast to the builders and tenantry. 'Seven hundred people ate themselves three parts dead,' he wrote exaggeratedly.

The following year building continued apace. Wyatt exhibited the drawings at the Royal Academy. Then a spring gale tearing at the flag already flying on the tower brought the structure crashing to the

Lee Priory, Kent, built by James Wyatt in the 1780s. From a drawing by J. P. Neale in *Views of Seats* (1826).

ground. Beckford and Wyatt were undeterred by this small setback. A new compo-cement, supposed to be everlasting, was chosen, and another tower was started. In 1798 the name Fonthill Abbey was finally adopted for what was eventually to be Beckford's sole residence. He intended according to an entry in Farington's diary (22nd December) that his own coffin should be placed in a special 'Revelation Chamber' with walls five feet thick and floor of jasper, to be viewed by pilgrims through a wire grating. He would be venerated as a sort of Apostle of the Arts in this sacred fane, designed to resemble a Catholic cathedral in Protestant England. Public rumours were rife. *The Gentleman's Magazine* had announced in 1796 that the top of the tower would command views 'near 80 miles every way'; and that, notwithstanding the great height, a coach and six could be driven from the base to summit and down again. In actual fact the tower at this date was a fairly squat affair which carried a spirelet like a candle snuffer. It was an adaptation of that feature with which Wyatt had crowned the central octagon at Lee Priory, Kent in the 1780s. Beckford kept to his resolution and allowed no one within the Barrier. In 1798 the existing wooden model of the Abbey was probably begun, to be continued when the additional east wing was started in 1812. In 1799, back from Portugal for the last time and determined to 'abjure the world' by shutting himself within the Fonthill grounds for ever, Beckford was furious to find so little progress made during his absence. He so

44

galvanized the dilatory architect into activity that he botched the job. In May 1800 part of the tower (and candle snuffer) again collapsed in a gale and Wyatt was forced to put all his other commitments aside and rebuild it in time for a prearranged visit to Fonthill by Nelson the following December.

To have hooked Nelson, the nation's darling, as a visitor for Christmas was a tremendous coup for the *déclassé* Beckford. He made the most of it. Nelson was in 1800 granted leave home after a long absence overseas. He was in poor health. He was also passionately in love with Emma, the notorious second wife of Beckford's kinsman, Sir William Hamilton. It was through the Hamiltons, from whom the great little sailor would for no considerations of propriety be separated, that Nelson's consent was obtained. Besides he was bound on a triumphal tour of the west and Fonthill was a convenient halting place. Furthermore he had been staying with the Hamiltons in the London house which Beckford had lent them. Tactfully the host had declined to do the honours in town, giving as an excuse his detestation of society and bustle, and really not wishing to lay himself open to snubs. He assured the Hamiltons that if Nelson accompanied them to Fonthill there would be no 'drawing room parasites' to molest them. Indeed there were not, for the simple reason that had any been invited they would not have accepted. Instead, Beckford's house guests were a handful of artists and men of letters.

Fonthill Abbey in 1799, from a watercolour by J. M. W. Turner. The short buttressed spire resembles that built by Wyatt at Lee Priory, Kent.

The distinguished party stayed in Splendens from 20th to 24th December. The Abbey was by no means finished, or fit for habitation. Of the ultimate cruciform building only the west and south arms with their appendages and the great tower and octagon saloon under it were anything like ready. Nevertheless Beckford entertained his guests on their last night at a great banquet in the Abbey. It was the first ceremony of any kind to be held there. John Britton and *The Gentleman's Magazine* gave detailed descriptions of what took place; how at five o'clock at dusk a long carriage procession moved from Splendens through the grounds between rows of loyal locals lined up to cheer the conquering hero, and brass bands playing *Rule Britannia*. The trees were festooned with lamps, and the Vice-Admiral's flag was flying from the tower. Indoors hooded figures held lighted torches. After a conducted tour through the rooms for the guests to admire the treasures, and a collation which Lucullus would have envied, Lady Hamilton obliged the company by impersonating Agrippina bearing the ashes of Germanicus in a golden urn. Her audience decorously shed tears.

In spite of Beckford's pride in having received Nelson at Fonthill and his dutiful speeches of congratulation, it does not seem that he found the Admiral companionable. He complained years afterwards that Nelson 'saw all with silent interest'; but then architecture and works of art could not be numbered among the Admiral's tastes. It also made Beckford not a little scornful that while being driven one afternoon through the grounds in his host's phaeton the hero of all those sea battles begged Beckford to let him get down. His nerves could not stand it, he declared; and he returned to the house on foot. Not does it seem that Nelson much cared for Beckford. He was rather shocked by an extraordinary proposal made by Beckford that Sir William Hamilton, who was not a rich man, should in return for an allowance of £2,000 a year from him, apply to the Crown for a peerage to be granted in remainder to him, Beckford. Nelson's comment to Emma on this scheme was that it was 'dirty' and a 'rub-off'. He certainly declined a second invitation to stay, but when Beckford invited himself to dine with Nelson in his house at Merton, the Admiral let him come. Perhaps the remarks committed by his young nephew to a diary reflected the uncle's impressions. Beckford was on the occasion too talkative. He praised his own musical compositions too much. And when he played extempore on the harpsichord, accompanying his own singing, the boy called it 'a very horrible noise'.

Not until 1807 however was the Abbey fit for habitation, and even then it was still far from finished. In the summer Beckford was able to move into the south wing while the north wing was being decorated. By September of the following year the octagon under the central tower was still an unadorned shell. Beckford was obliged to present Wyatt with an ultimatum that unless the octagon was finished by the thirtieth of the month he would cease all building forthwith and sack him, contractors,

Nelson's reception at Fonthill in December 1800. He stayed at Splendens and was escorted to the unfinished Abbey for an evening banquet (described in *The Gentlemen's Magazine*, April, 1801).

builders and workmen. The threat acted like a charm. A tremendous bustle ensued. By 11th September the inside of the tower lantern was stuccoed, and Beckford wrote to the absent Franchi, 'The great central rose will be in place today before dinner.' It was. On the 15th the fan vaulting was in hand. On the 16th he told Franchi:

Wyatt's wooden model, begun 1798 and continued in 1812.

The atrocious neglect by the great Cloaca cannot lightly be forgiven. If he comes now, it will be to see what are, perhaps, irremediable mistakes. It is true that I have some knowledge of my own, but not enough, and not to that extent which a task like the octagon, so imperiously demands.

On the 18th: 'All three of the Batalha windows are already in place and produce the most splendid effect.' This was a reference to the stained glass windows being inserted within three of the great arches of the octagon which ran from the floor to the Nunnery arcade. The windows were probably adapted from the sanctuary windows of Batalha Abbey, which

47

The Octagon or Saloon under the tower. From this central apartment the four wings of the Abbey extended. View from J. Storer's *A Description of Fonthill* (1812).

Beckford had seen in 1794 and which had been measured and drawn by J. C. Murphy for his splendid book on the Portuguese abbey, published in 1795. They do not however accord with those of the Capela do Fundador which was without question the inspiration of the Fonthill octagon. A watercolour of the Abbey by Turner, shown on p 45 and based on Wyatt's earlier project, shows that the octagon down to, or rather up to, the curved flying buttresses exactly resembled the Batalha chapel. The glass to which Beckford was referring had been made by Francis Eginton of Birmingham and his son William Raphael, from designs of William Hamilton, R.A., the historical and heraldic painter. Francis Eginton had invented a process of painting and staining glass which resulted in a brilliant translucency. In all, the Egintons provided an immense amount of glass for the Abbey to the tune of £12,000. On the 25th Beckford wrote: 'Yesterday they did five of the great circular windows [those above the

48

Nunnery arcade, taken from the Batalha chapter house], today they finish the other three.'

Beckford was in his zenith. He was constantly with John Dixon, Wyatt's able assistant, and George Hayter, the clerk of works. His description (quoted by Mr. Boyd Alexander) of the scene from a vantage point, ninety feet up in the Nunnery arcade, bubbles with enthusiasm and excitement:

'It's really stupendous, the spectacle here at night' – he wrote to Franchi, 'the number of people at work, lit up by lads; the innumerable torches suspended everywhere, the immense and endless spaces, the gulph below; above, the gigantic spider's web of scaffolding – especially when, standing under the finished and numberless arches of the galleries, I listen to the reverberating voices in the stillness of the night, and see immense buckets of plaster and water ascending, as if they were drawn up from the bowels of a mine, amid shouts from subterranean depths, oaths from Hell itself, and chanting from Pandemonium or the synagogue . . .'

Until the autumn of 1809 the tower remained encased in the 'spider's web of scaffolding'. And only in 1813 was the eastern transept built with its end turrets copied from those of the entrance gateway to St. Augustine's monastery at Canterbury, which dates from the early fourteenth century. After Wyatt's sudden death that year in a coach accident Beckford lost interest in the east wing which he never properly finished.

As for Splendens Beckford had by 1806 made up his mind irrevocably to pull it down. His cousin and future son-in-law the Marquess of Douglas begged him piteously to spare what was a classical masterpiece. But he would listen neither to him nor to Wyatt, who to his credit deprecated its demolition. He told the latter he ought not to heed the world's opinion any more than he himself did. In 1807 Splendens (apart from one pavilion which survived until 1921) fell to the house-breakers. A seven-day sale had already taken place of those contents deemed by their volatile owner unsuited to a mock medieval monastery.

Of all England's great country houses which have long ago disappeared Beckford's Gothic Fonthill Abbey is about the best known to us. From the innumerable plans, coloured plates, engravings and paintings of the outside and inside, not to mention the books, such as James Storer's (1812), John Britton's (1823) and John Rutter's (1823), exclusively devoted to the place, we can find our way round the grounds, the gardens and the rooms, identifying each stained glass window, each carpet, pair of curtains and stick of furniture, and practically each picture and precious object of virtu, to use a phrase much favoured by Beckford. It has long been customary for architectural historians to criticize Fonthill Abbey because of its inconvenience as a dwelling, if not to deride its scale and styles as the vulgar concept of an eccentric millionaire not quite in his right senses. Perceptive critics of today find in it one of the most interesting and sublime expressions of the English Romantic movement.

ABOVE A cartoon by William Hamilton, R.A. for a stained glass window at Fonthill Abbey, now in the Victoria and Albert Museum.

49

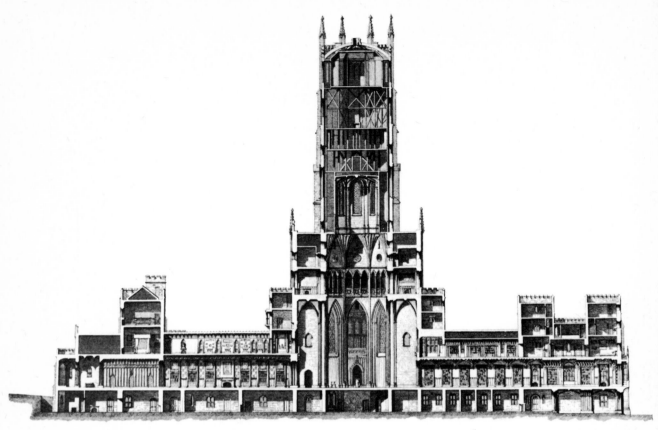

Longitudinal section of Fonthill
Abbey, taken from John
Rutter's *Delineations of Fonthill*
(1823).

OPPOSITE Plan of Fonthill
Abbey, taken from John
Rutter's *Delineations of Fonthill*.

Fonthill Abbey, lithograph view
from the north-west by John
Buckler.

FONTHILL ABBEY.

Plate 2.

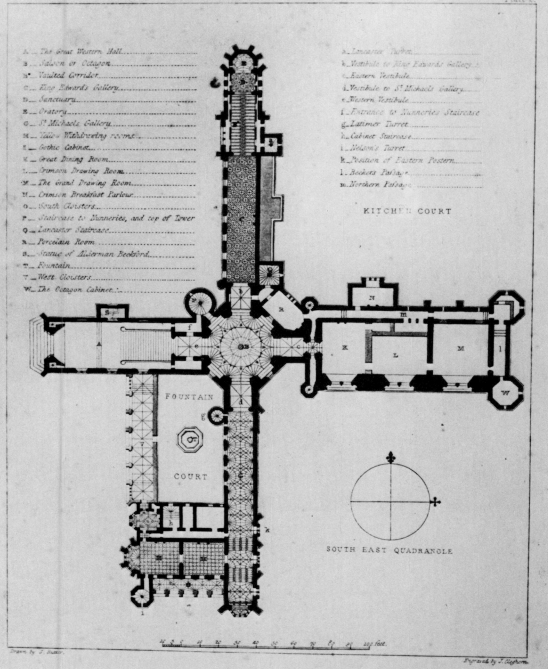

A. The Great Western Hall
B. Saloon or Octagon
c. Vaulted Corridor
C. King Edwards Gallery
D. Sanctuary
E. Oratory
G. St Michaels Gallery
H. Yellow Withdrawing rooms
I. Gothic Cabinet
K. Great Dining Room
L. Crimson Drawing Room
M. The Grand Drawing Room
N. Crimson Breakfast Parlour
O. South Cloisters
P. Staircase to Nunneries, and top of Tower
Q. Lancaster Staircase
R. Porcelain Room
S. Statue of Alderman Beckford
T. Fountain
U. West Cloisters
W. The Octagon Cabinet

a. Lancaster Turret
b. Vestibule to King Edwards Gallery
c. Eastern Vestibule
d. Vestibule to St Michaels Gallery
e. Western Vestibule
f. Entrance to Nunneries Staircase
g. Latimer Turret
h. Cabinet Staircase
i. Nelsons Turret
k. Position of Eastern Postern
l. Beckets Passage
m. Northern Passage

KITCHEN COURT

FOUNTAIN COURT

SOUTH EAST QUADRANGLE

Drawn by J. Buder.   Engraved by J. Cleghorn.

PLAN OF THE PRINCIPAL STORY.

The dotted lines represent the Ornamented Ceilings Groining &c.

Hadlow Castle tower, Kent, by Walter Barton May (1838–40). Together with Eaton Hall, this is one of the many domestic buildings influenced by Fonthill Abbey.

The charge so frequently levelled that Fonthill Abbey did not make a suitable residence cannot of course be gainsaid. It was preposterously, absurdly uncomfortable even in the days when indoor servants were employed by the hundred. The kitchen was seemingly miles away from the Oak Parlour where Beckford habitually dined; the eighteen bedrooms, reached by several twisted staircases of inordinate height, were practically inaccessible. Thirteen were so small, poky and lacking ventilation as to be unusable. In winter and even in summer all the rooms were as cold as tombs, so that sixty fires had to be kept burning practically throughout the year, There were no bells in the house. Instead bevies of servants were posted outside every door. There were no stables or coach-houses, only a few sheds for Beckford's carriage and ponies, for he chose to hire post horses when he travelled to London. But these and all other practical shortcomings are beside the point. Beckford was perfectly well aware of them the moment he decided to turn his folly into his home. Fonthill Abbey was intended, to quote Nikolaus Pevsner, 'to create sentiments of amazement, of shock, even of awe.' And so it succeeded. Above all it was intended to convey a scenic effect of ineffable, dream-like beauty. Like a dream it arose, and like a dream it was extinguished.

That Fonthill Abbey was considered by nearly all those people who saw it – and most of them held Beckford in very low esteem – to be a singularly sublime building is incontrovertible. Contemporary artists flocked to paint it – W. Finley, C. F. Porden, T. Higham, J. Le Keux, J. P. Neale, C. Wild, G. Cattermole, J. Buckler, John Martin and J. M. W. Turner, who made seven watercolours at least, and was haunted by the astonishing structure rising from a bower of trees on the edge of the forbidding downs. Constable, who loathed the landed classes, raved about it, calling it 'a romantic place, quite fairy land'. And Cobbett, who loathed them hardly less, wrote, 'After that sight, all sights become mean until that be out of the mind.' In fine weather, according to contemporaries it was ethereal, in bad weather it was demonic, veering from one swift mood to another like its mercurial creator. In short, it became a legend to young artists and architects, and was the inspiration of many houses of a later generation like Coleorton, Toddington, Childwall, Eastnor, Lowther, (W. Porden's) Eaton and Hadlow, to name only a few, besides Barry and Pugin's Houses of Parliament.

The very measurements of this unusual cruciform country house are stupendous. From the north to south the length was 312 feet, being that of the nave and sanctuary of Westminster Abbey; from west to east 270 feet. The height of the two octagonal turrets of the east transept was 120 feet and that of the great central tower 276 feet. To understand at what distance it was visible we have only to bear in mind that the base of the tower was 278 feet higher than the tip of Salisbury cathedral spire. Had the Fonthill spire, projected by Wyatt in 1799 and shown in Wild's conjectural watercolour, been attempted (and had it ever stood up to the

gales) the vision of verticality presented would have been without parallel in the world.

Notwithstanding the applause of discerning artists and writers, Beckford, who was seldom satisfied with anything for long, himself criticized the building on aesthetic grounds (quite apart from its physical inconvenience). Through his mouthpiece Rutter he gave his reasons. 'Though the general effect is magnificent,' he conceded, 'the composition as a work of art is exceedingly faulty. A want of balance, harmony, and keeping in the great masses; no breadth of chiaro-oscuro, no repose but a uniform sparkling of light from the number of facettes into which the surface is cut.' He realized that the addition of the east transept 'crushed every other part.' The great elevation of the west doorway 'reduced to mouse-trap dimensions the apertures of the cloisters, of the arcade,' he said, and the lack of buttresses against the south façade and the feebleness of those of the tower were a serious shortcoming. How true as things turned out! No one but the house's creator (certainly not the twenty-five-year-old Quaker author from Shaftesbury to whom he had supplied information) would have dared be so censorious. 'Disproportion prevails in every part of the exterior. The beauty of contour is entirely absent.' The last sentence is an unjustifiable stricture, when we judge the building from the south and west, from which most of the illustrations were taken. For from whatever angle it was viewed, the accidental juxtaposition of towers, turrets, gables, pinnacles, oriels and arcades was superlative in picturesque terms. Yet the Beckford-Rutter passage modestly admitted, 'The Abbey cannot be contemplated without emotions that have never been excited by any building erected by any private individual in our times.' I should think not. And was not Rutter perhaps writing without

53

dictation the final words, 'the Abbey can be judged of by no common rules'?

When J. C. Loudon looked at the ruins in 1833 he was appalled by the poor quality of the workmanship and shoddiness of the material used. He said the remaining walls were part brick, part stone, part studwork and the mortar could be picked out in powder by a finger. 'Long strings of tarred packthread [were] hanging from nails' – as though the work had been done by men in a state of intoxication, which they too often were, plied by Beckford with ale and spirits. He said that the Roman cement used gave the texture an insubstantial appearance. How true was this? The closest surviving parallel to Fonthill is Wyatt's Ashridge Park, begun while he was still engaged on the Abbey. The surface of Ashridge, and also the ashlar skin of that fragment of Fonthill which stands, looks solid

A letter from William Beckford to James Wyatt, dated 23rd December 1811.

enough today, though rather smooth and lifeless. But it cannot be denied that the walls of the Lancaster State Bedroom now stripped of its oak wainscot and damask hangings are a precarious compound of ashlar, rubble and brick. And the newel post of the twisting stair in the Lancaster Tower, meant to appear a solid tree bole, gives out a hollow ring when tapped. When Mr. Lansdown visited the scene in 1844 however he found the quality of what remained even finer than the engravings of Rutter and Britton had led him to suppose.

Beckford always stressed that the merits of the Abbey must be assessed in relation to the grounds; that the two made one work of art and could not be divorced. Certainly he was the first to carry out on a large scale the teaching of Uvedale Price's *Essay on the Picturesque*, first published in 1794. And here it is not inopportune to refer to Beckford's attitude to landscape and his love of plants and flowers.

Beneath the poetic descriptions of scenery, to which he gave rein in his journals and letters, whether the English Lake District, the Alps, the

John Martin's view of the South front of the Abbey, showing the east wing added in 1811. To the left of the door is the Cloister walk, which darkened the Oak Parlour behind it. The Great Western Hall projects to the left of the picture.

55

Roman Campagna or the carob groves of Estremadura – and he claimed that he always looked at nature with the eye of a painter – we discern the experienced botanist and arboriculturist's down-to-earth practical knowledge. For instance, in June 1782 Beckford observed how the turf around Innsbrück was 'enamelled' with wild flowers. 'A sort of bluebell predominated, brighter than ultramarine; here and there auriculas looked out of the moss.' In Portugal one June he listed the wild flowers along the road verges by their proper names – *Papaver corniculatum* and *Lupinus luteus*. His taste in the choicest hothouse plants was no less discerning. On the death in 1810 of Princess Amelia he ordered his agent to lose no time in buying up to £100 worth of the finest oleander and myrtle shrubs at the sale of her effects. In July of the same year he sent his daughter a present of the scarlet *Nerine curvifolia*, then known as *Amaryllis Fothergillii*. He lamented that the prevalent craze for novelty made it impossible to get the good old plants, jasmines, gardenias, etc., 'in the condition in which one ought to have them', and that the beautiful *Dolichos*, a genus of sub-shrub, called the shrub-bean, was unobtainable from the nurserymen.

On the whole Beckford preferred common, native shrubs and trees to the exotic specimens. In the same way he liked parks to retain an air of naturalness, preferring the sublime to the fashionable taste for the orderly. He disliked Cirencester Park because of its formality, its dead straight, radiating rides leading nowhere, and its lack of diversity and water. On a second visit to Aranjuez in Spain he was greatly distressed by the wild garden having been tamed, the terraces levelled, banks smoothed and shrubs cut into genteel shapes. Of all European gardens his favourite was the Boboli in Florence because it was a wilderness with a classical frame. Although he had in his library all Repton's books, he disapproved of Repton's and his master Capability Brown's shaven, rounded edges, their artificial clumps, and spotty punctuations. He politely but flatly turned down Repton's request to 'improve' Fonthill.

In addition to Uvedale Price's *Essay*, another considerable influence on Beckford's layout of his two gardens at Fonthill and in Bath was the famous garden made between 1740 and 1775 by his great-uncle Charles Hamilton at Painshill. Walpole called Painshill the perfect example of the savage Alpine garden. 'All is great and foreign and rude; the walks seem not designed but cut through the woods and pines.' Hamilton was one of the first exponents of the Picturesque landscape school, a fact recognized by Price who acknowledged that 'Mr. Hamilton, who created Painshill, not only had studied pictures, but had studied them with the express purpose of improving real landscape. The place he created . . . fully proves the use of such a study.' Beckford in turn accepted Price's emphatic advocacy that a study of the Old Masters best indicated how a landowner ought to dispose his trees and water. He endorsed Price's written recommendation of the desirability of roughness, sudden variation and irregularity, as in unadorned nature. Price's teaching did not imply that

the attempt ought to or could be made to reproduce actual landscape paintings, but that the principles of composition, the feeling for colour, light and shade might well derive from a select few. It is just possible that of these select few in Beckford's case were two exquisite little Elsheimers of *Tobias and the Angel* which he owned at different times. The first, known as the *Large Tobias*, had been bought by his father and was sold in 1802 by the son, who regretting his action then managed to buy a slightly earlier version, called the *Little Tobias*, a minute painting no bigger than a man's hand. In the landscape of the *Large Tobias* we can detect features – namely in the margin of the lake blurred by wild flowers, the steep wooded bank behind the lake, and even the tower rising in the background – which in years to come Beckford, consciously or unconsciously, was to reproduce, albeit in an entirely different genre, at Fonthill Abbey.

Beckford began by ruthlessly scrapping the formal layout of Splendens, leaving not a memory behind of that classic seat, if we exclude the 'Jones' gateway, lake and boathouse. He boasted in old age that his greatest achievement at Fonthill was the creation of a flowering wilderness round the Abbey, his intention being that the art which had contributed to its

Tobias and the Angel, by Adam Elsheimer (1578–1610), now in the National Gallery and once in Beckford's ownership. Did the lake in the foreground and the landscape in the background suggest to him Bitham Lake and the American Plantation?

Distant view of Fonthill Abbey from the east with stone quarry in the foreground, by J. M. W. Turner.

creation should be concealed. The main approach to the Abbey was by the Great Western Avenue three-quarters of a mile long. Even so the avenue was not composed of one species of tree planted at regular intervals in two straight lines. On the contrary it consisted of a variety of trees and shrubs of all kinds, planted in clumps so as to form on each side 'an impervious thicket'. The broad, somewhat irregular green ride which was left between gave the illusion of having been cut by early monks out of a primeval forest. As the avenue approached the Abbey it widened. The building thus gradually loomed into sight against a crepuscular background of dark firs and oaks. The arrangement was calculated, especially at night time by full moon, to accord with a romantic recollection in Price's *Essay:*

All the characteristic beauties of the avenue, its solemn stillness, the religious awe its inspires, are greatly heightened by moon light. This I once very strongly experienced in approaching a venerable castle-like mansion built in the beginning of the 15th century; a few gleams had pierced the deep gloom of the avenue; a large massive tower at the end of it, seen through a long perspective, and half lit by the uncertain beams of the moon, had a grand mysterious effect. Suddenly a light appeared in the tower; then as suddenly its twinkling vanished . . . again more lights quickly shifted to different parts of the building

58

and the whole scene most forcibly brought to my fancy the times of fairies and chivalry.

This was just what appealed to Beckford. Actually the Fonthill scene must have been more often witnessed by his gardeners who were made to mow the Great Western Avenue, the intersecting Beacon Terrace and the Clerk's Walk running north-west from the Abbey, by night.

Throughout the grounds Beckford was very careful to isolate specimen trees among ordinary, native trees, as though they had found a way there naturally. He wanted the common trees and shrubs indigenous to the country to predominate, like Scotch fir, oak, birch and a smattering of larch. For undergrowth he encouraged hazel, holly, thorn and even furze. Loudon during his visit in 1833 was immensely impressed by the apparent naturalness of the grounds. He said it was the only garden in England

in which you will find the most perfect unity of character preserved throughout the grounds, and that character one belonging to an age long since passed in this country, and only now to be found in certain mountainous regions of Catholic countries on the continent.

There was not a single gravel walk or made road, or in the vicinity of the house a single specimen tree bar an apricot and a fig tree planted against the south entrance, 'as we may suppose by some monk who had brought the seeds of these fruits from some Italian or Swiss monastery.'

To the south of the small plateau on which the Abbey stood – and it is amazing how so spread a building fitted into so circumscribed an area – the land dropped steeply. Below a terrace was the American Garden, a shrubbery of mauve rhododendrons, white magnolias, azaleas, arbutus, Portugal laurel and the Carolina rose. Here flourished also the Angelica tree (*Aralia*) the Andromeda shrub, the Yulan tree (*Magnolia denudata*) and the Carolina Allspice (*Calycanthus floridus*). This shrubbery of sophisticated planting, intersected by winding paths, bordered with English and foreign heaths, which led to the Norwegian log hut, melted, when seen from the distance, into the surrounding groves, and sloped westward into Bitham Lake. The lake was excavated and dammed by Beckford with consummate artifice. 'The lake looks', he wrote, 'as if God had made it, it is so natural, without the least trace of art . . . it spreads itself grandiosely, and the swans look as if they are in Paradise.' In fashioning this jagged and islanded sheet of water Beckford had in mind perhaps the enchanted gardens of Tasso, perhaps Milton's *Paradise Lost*, or perhaps his little Elsheimer landscape of *Tobias and the Angel*. Today the lake, swathed in rampaging ponticum and overshadowed by oaks and chestnuts, lies dark and almost unapproachable below a steep bank of spiky fir trees, densely regimented. But from the large, flat rocks which jut from the south bank Turner and a host of artists used to sketch the most dramatic of all views of the fairy Abbey hovering over the misty water, its walls tinged pink by the western sun, its window panes sparkling like a cascade of diamonds.

Turner sketching, from a drawing by C. Martin.

59

Statue of Alderman Beckford by
J. F. Moore. It originally stood
in a niche of the Great Western
Hall of Fonthill Abbey.

5·STUCCO HALLS

THE state entry to the Abbey was by way of the transept which faced the straight but undulating Great Western Avenue. The pointed doorway, under an arch adorned with snail-like crockets, was taken from the principal entrance to Batalha's monastic church. Above it and within a canopy flanked by slender finials the figure of St. Antony of Padua in the attitude of preaching was carved in grey-green Chilmark stone by the sculptor Joseph Theakston. It can be seen today in the garden of Wardour Castle. The figure is much worn but the weather-pocked face is sad, ascetic and holy. The oak door valves, each thirty-five feet high and weighing more than a ton, were so beautifully hinged that they were effortlessly opened by the Swiss dwarf Perro, dressed in 'gold and embroidery'. An impression of the doors' immensity was accentuated by his tiny and grotesque figure.

The lofty hall behind the doors was at first intended to be a banqueting room, but like others at Fonthill developed into something different. The walls were of pink plaster. The great hammer-beam roof bore painted oak shields of the various heiresses from whom Beckford supposed he was descended. Three tall south windows filled with the Egintons' painted glass illuminated a full length marble figure (by J. F. Moore) of Alderman Beckford. He was made to stand within a facing alcove in the act of declaiming like the Commendatore in *Don Giovanni*. A wide stone staircase led to the central Octagon. The entrance hall at Ashridge Park also has a hammer-beam roof and minstrels' gallery extending the whole width of the room.

The day to day entrance to the Abbey however was by the Eastern Postern Tower in the south transept. A rather insignificant door opened to the ground floor and those comparatively small rooms jutting out westwards which Beckford used when he was alone. One of them on the ground floor behind the South Cloisters was the Oak Parlour. It was made somewhat dark and gloomy by the colonnade which shaded the south windows and by the oblique cross light coming from the west oriel window. Moreover the ceiling was low and the walls were hung with family portraits and tapestry. Below the portraits concealed doors in the wainscot opened into water-closets. When alone or with a few hangers-on Beckford dined in the Oak Parlour, always in state. In the projecting Nelson Turret a winding stairway led to the floor above. It contained the adjacent Yellow Withdrawing Rooms over the Oak Parlour, and the Gothic Cabinet with walls of green silk, inset mirrors and ceiling of fan tracery. A doorway opened on to the upper open walk of the West Cloisters, bounding the Fountain Court.

60

A doorway from the Eastern Yellow Withdrawing Room led directly into the southern end of St. Michael's Gallery. This was the way Beckford liked to direct his guests in order that they might be confronted and impressed by the tremendous enfilade of apartments running in an unbroken line to the far end of the north wing. Indeed the vista was breath-taking, whether viewed from the south oriel of St. Michael's Gallery or the other way round. At night time the vista from north to south was rendered doubly spectacular by an avenue of lighted candles and lamps. The large glass panes of the south oriel window, when the curtains were drawn back, reflected the twinkling lights so that the length of the enfilade appeared twice what it actually was. The Gallery ceiling, in stucco, only fifteen feet high, was fan-vaulted, painted and jointed to resemble stonework. The walls above the oak wainscoting were washed buff or palest pink. The crimson carpet – crimson being the Hamilton livery colour – was specially woven with Hamilton cinquefoils. Bookcases

LEFT The Great Western Hall seen from the Octagon. A drawing by John Storer, published in the *Portfolio*, vol. I, 1823.

RIGHT The entrance hall at Ashridge Park, by James Wyatt, which resembles the Great Western Hall at Fonthill Abbey.

61

Stained glass window of Thomas à Becket designed by Benjamin West for Becket's passage in the east transept of Fonthill Abbey. Bought in the 1823 sale by Bristol Corporation and now in the Lord Mayor's Chapel.

and windows were partly concealed by scarlet draperies on brass rods. The curtains were royal blue with gold gatherings, borders and hems. The figures of the Fathers of the Church, in addition to the Venerable Bede and Roger Bacon in the Egintons' multi-coloured windows, were designed by William Hamilton and Benjamin West. Nothing revealed so clearly the divergent tastes of patron and architect as the decoration of the Fonthill interior, which was almost wholly Beckford's. Whereas Wyatt, who prided himself on a correct understanding of the English Gothic style, would invariably, when left to his own devices, use pastel shades, and at boldest a Pompeian red, Beckford, who thought nothing of mixing continental with English styles, favoured the conjunction of exotic crimson, scarlet, purple and gold decoration. Such oriental colour schemes were at least twenty years in advance of the Prince Regent's decoration of the Brighton Pavilion.

Close up of the south-east side of the Abbey by John Storer.

62

Above St. Michael's Gallery were the Vaulted Library, the Yellow Chintz Boudoir, and the founder of the Abbey's ascetic cell. This was a poky little chamber over the south oriel, containing a truckle bed without hangings, the sparsest furniture and no fireplace.

The far end of St Michael's Gallery was bounded by a glazed Gothic screen, the arched doors of which, usually kept open, led through the South Vestibule to the Grand Saloon or Octagon. Four high and narrow vestibules and the Octagon formed the base of the central tower. Whereas the height of the vestibules, empty and in Rutter's words, 'chalky and cold . . . harsh and unpleasing', occupied four storeys, that of the Octagon occupied six. The effect of this apartment must have been astounding. Eight attenuated pointed openings gave access to the four arms of the Abbey, three windows and the Tower Staircase. The walls were of a rough sandy finish, a simple background to long scarlet hangings below the windows reaching down to the floor. The windows were suggested by

St. Michael's Gallery, occupying the whole south wing of the Abbey with oriel window at the end. The ceiling was fan-vaulted, and the windows were filled with painted glass. Crimson carpet and curtains of crimson and royal blue trimmed with gold.

63

King Edward's Gallery in the
north wing. Contained portraits
of Edward III and Beckford's
Gartered ancestors. In the
middle stood the Borghese
Palace table of *pietre commesse*,
now at Charlecote Park,
Warwickshire.

Murphy's book on Batalha, as was the vaulting originally. According to a
sketch of Wyatt's, dated 1796, the fourteenth-century octagon roof of the
Founder's Chapel at Batalha was Beckford's chosen prototype. H. A. N.
Brockman however believes that Wyatt, who had not seen Batalha and
was presumably reluctant to reproduce a foreign roof, turned to Ely
Cathedral for the final adjustment, since it is the only English cathedral to
have an octagon crossing. At all events the vault to be carried out was of
the Perpendicular variety which Wyatt preferred to all others. Over the
entrance to the east wing was an organ loft where Beckford and Franchi
delighted to play by the hour. Again, the only apartment in England to give us
some idea of the height and scale of the Fonthill Octagon is Wyatt's square
staircase hall at Ashridge.

Over the great openings of the Octagon ran an arcade in the Early
English style. Wyatt's gamut of medieval styles at Fonthill was deliberately

meant to induce an authentic Gothic flavour. Behind the arcade were the so-called Nunneries whose only protection from the chasm below was a stone balustrade. In 1802 Beckford, enraged at finding that Wyatt had put up a balustrade without consulting him about the design, lent against a pier and with all his force kicked the stonework on to the paving and the furniture below. On the floor above the Nunneries, and on a level with the pendentives of the lantern, were bedrooms, reached by a fatiguing ascent up the circular turret, at the north-west angle of the Octagon. From the north-east angle of the principal floor the Porcelain Room was entered.

The North Vestibule led to King Edward's Gallery, which was some two-thirds the length of St Michael's Gallery, being 127 feet long and 17 feet wide. It was named after Edward III from whom, through John of Gaunt, Beckford was descended. It was lit by a row of seven west windows. Curtains and hangings from brass rods between the bookcases on the east wall were of purple and scarlet. The walls were covered with a flowered red damask. The ceiling of dark oak was compartmented in Gothic panels. Emblazoned shields adorned the handsome frieze and gilded cornice. Over a reddish alabaster chimneypiece, whence specially 'perfum'd coal' according to Samuel Rogers 'produc'd the brightest flame,' hung a full-length portrait of Edward III copied by Matthew Cotes Wyatt from the one at Windsor. Quarter-length portraits of Beckford's Gartered ancestors hung over the bookcases. In the middle of this room stood the huge table, now at Charlecote Park, of which the slab of *pietre commesse*, with oval centre in oriental onyx, said to be the largest onyx in the world, and surrounded by jaspers and breccia marbles, came from the Borghese Palace in Rome. The elaborate oak base was designed by Beckford who had a habit of adding feet of this rather incongruous wood to classical furniture. The four little oak tables in the windows, also now at Charlecote, were likewise designed by him, as were the pair of Elizabethan-style court cupboards with bulbous supports to a heavy

The south elevation of the Mausoleum of King John I at Batalha.

The table from King Edward's Gallery, now at Charlecote Park, has a central onyx, the largest in the world. The oak base was provided by Beckford.

Ebony state bed, now at Charlecote Park, with original crimson hangings, formerly in the Lancaster State Bedroom at Fonthill Abbey.

Augsburg cabinet of 1550–60, called by Beckford, who had the base made, the 'Holbein cabinet'. Now in the Victoria and Albert Museum.

canopy. These astonishing objects were just the sort of furniture which the Victorians were to fake in the 1860s and '70s.

Admittedly the romantic in Beckford sometimes overcame his probity. He pretended that the ebony state bed (it too is at Charlecote, having been purchased with the other things there by George Lucy at the Fonthill sale of 1822), which is palpably seventeenth century, had belonged to Henry VII; that some ebony chairs, likewise seventeenth century and made in the East Indies, were once Cardinal Wolsey's; and that the Augsburg cabinet of 1550–60, of which the base was made for him, was designed by Holbein who died in 1543. He was too good a connoisseur not to know that these pretensions were absurd. He told visitors that a pair of carved gilt and painted coffers, kept in the Sanctuary at Fonthill Abbey (and now in the Wallace Collection), were of James I's reign, whereas they were almost certainly designed by and made for himself.

Next in the enfilade came the Vaulted Corridor. It was purposely kept gloomy and mysterious in anticipation of the blaze of illumination of the holy of holies to come. It had no windows visible from inside. Light filtered obliquely through latticed recesses like confessionals from the windows in the outer walls. The coved ceiling of gilded cross bands was to some visitors the most beautiful in the house. The floor was covered with a Persian carpet of extraordinary size. Otherwise the room was empty. The Sanctuary was raised a step above the floor of the Corridor. It was entered under a curtain over folding doors which by some ingenious device were drawn back when Beckford, pronouncing the magic word 'Open',

66

stamped on a plank in the floor. The walls were covered with crimson damask in a large honeysuckle pattern. From the honeycomb ceiling hung pendants like stalactites which made the little chamber resemble Aladdin's cave. The pair of gilt and painted coffers which I have just referred to, stood against the walls. They are of sandalwood, the sides and lids carved in a diamond pattern enclosing fleurs-de-lys and the Tudor rose.

Finally, at the extreme end of the north wing was the culminating goal, the Oratory, its floor again slightly raised. From the ceiling ribs gleaming with purple, scarlet and gold a silvergilt lamp was suspended. Two large

The Sanctuary and Oratory were the termination of the north wing. The pair of sandalwood coffers are now in the Wallace Collection. A silver gilt lamp hung above the figure of St. Antony of Padua by Rossi. The looking glass was inserted by Beckford's successor. From J. P. Neale's *Views of Seats*, 2nd series, vol. I (1824).

silver candelabra flanked an altar covered with a Persian carpet of figured silk. Upon it stood the alabaster figure of St. Antony of Padua with the child Christ in his arms by the sculptor J. C. F. Rossi. A profusion of enamelled reliquaries and jewelled monstrances gave a truly Catholic air to the altar. On all these treasures the Egintons' painted windows, partly veiled by rich hangings of purple, crimson and gold, cast a dim, religious light. The sanctity of the shrine was enhanced by generous wafts of incense and distant peals of the organ reverberating down the galleries.

Above the suite of rooms in the north wing were the long Lancaster Picture Gallery, the Lancaster State Bedroom, containing the ebony state bed with crimson damask hangings (now at Charlecote), and the Duke and Duchess of Hamilton's Bedchambers.

The east wing was an afterthought, and a clumsy one at that. It was far wider, longer and bulkier than its opposite number, the west transept. Three gargantuan windows pierced the south wall and extended through two storeys of which the upper was left unfloored. Referring to their immense size and immense cost in a letter to Franchi in September 1817 Beckford wrote:

Fonthill from the south-east showing gigantic eastern transept. From Britton's *Fonthill*.

You can't imagine the torments we've undergone to prevent the whole Basilica and the great roof from falling on the heads of the workmen . . . T'was a mad and diabolic undertaking. What has been done passes belief and seems more than anything else to be the result of some pact and wager with Satan. Never has so much brick been used except at Babylon . . .

The whole business was of course the breath of life to him. But the decoration of the lower state rooms was never properly completed. The Great Dining Room and the Crimson Drawing Room led to the still vaster Grand Drawing Room. Ceiling beams left plain were carried by carved and gilded corbels. The walls of Garter blue damask were hung with pictures, not of the first order. A spiky Gothic overmantel mirror in triptych form was set over a chimneypiece, half Gothic and half classical. There were other indications in this room of Beckford's dawning interest in the neo-classical. The influence of Thomas Hope can be detected in the suite of sofa and chairs with winged gryphon arms, and backs formed of pilasters carrying pedimented top-rails. The magnificent Aubusson carpet had been specially woven in 1814 for St. Cloud by order of Napoleon. And in the window was placed Riesener's famous roll-top bureau. Beckford was

Grand Drawing Room, in the east wing. One of the last state rooms to be decorated. Walls of Garter blue damask. In the window is Riesener's *Bureau du Roi Stanislaus*. From Rutter's *Delineations* (1823).

69

'Peace to the Souls'. Beckford's design for a wall cupboard at Fonthill.

extremely particular how pictures and furniture should be arranged in a room. 'Everything depends on the way objects are placed, and where,' he wrote. 'Horrors in one place discount beauties in another.' Nothing must be left to chance. He even selected meticulously the species and colour of flowers he was arranging in a vase as though he were painting a still life.

The Octagon Cabinet, occupying one of the turrets at the extreme end of the East front, and the Crimson Breakfast Parlour, a lugubrious room facing north and used by Franchi as a sort of office, bring the apartments of the *piano nobile* of the Abbey to an end.

Over the long years Beckford's taste in pictures, works of art, furniture and decoration changed; and it is fascinating to trace its development. What is remarkable about his taste is not its coincidence with contemporary vogues, but its anticipation of fashions to come. As in his beliefs, his humour and his behaviour Beckford was often well ahead of his time. And all his life he was unashamedly drawn towards the extravagant in art.

Throughout the first and second decades of the nineteenth century Beckford's finances were becoming more and more embarrassed. His Jamaican sugar plantations were not paying and his estates, which he never once visited, were grossly mismanaged. His annual income of £155,000 in 1797 was reduced to £30,000 by 1805. That sounds enough in all conscience, but his extravagant living, purchases of works of art, and above all building, outstripped a sadly diminishing revenue. In 1807 he dared to get himself returned to Parliament (this time taking his own seat of Hindon), now that his arch-enemies Loughborough (elevated to the earldom of Rosslyn in 1801) and the younger Pitt were both dead. Extraordinary as it may seem to us he evidently entered the chamber of the House of Commons for the first time that year. There are no records of his ever having spoken or voted in Parliament.

Meanwhile very few people came to Fonthill. Beckford's seclusion and exclusion of visitors brought him a notoriety which tickled his vanity and increased his bitterness. His household consisted, apart from a regiment of ordinary servants, of Dr. Ehrhart, the Strasbourgian physician who had been with him in Portugal and who died in his service in 1807, the Abbé Denis Macquin, formerly Professor of Rhetoric and Belles Lettres at Meaux, topographer and heraldic draughtsman, and Franchi. By 1810 John ('Warwick') Smith, nicknamed Father Bestorum, the watercolour artist, had joined the little court. These men ate with him. In a humbler capacity but in constant attendance was the dwarf, called Perro, Pierrot and sometimes Nanibus. He was what may be termed a familiar servant in constant attendance. He remained with his master for forty years. He was a Swiss from Evian where Beckford had rescued him from wretched circumstances. He is constantly mentioned in Beckford's correspondence as an object of affectionate amusement. He had a grim, determined manner, was faithful, cunning, grubby and rather smelly.

70

These then were some of the dependants with whom Beckford felt at ease because his relations with them were not social. Farington observed that he 'is easy to professional men, but of consummate pride to people in higher stations'. Artists were usually welcome to stay as long as they wished. Benjamin West, to whom for several years Beckford paid a stipend in return for an annual supply of paintings, Turner, William Hamilton and Ozias Humphrey, from whom he bought occasional paintings, came to stay. So too did Henry Tresham, who combined painting with dealing in and repairing pictures. We are told that on 23rd December 1799 he 'magnificently framed, well-placed, and tenderly washed' the Altieri Claudes so that they appeared 'in the utmost glory and perfection'. Samuel Rogers was received in 1817 with every distinction. Beckford having learned that the poet was lodging at the local inn pressed him to dine at the Abbey two days running. Sir Isaac Heard, Garter King of Arms, and G. F. Beltz, Lancaster Herald, did not think their reputations compromised by lengthy correspondence and occasional visits. Besides, Beckford was a client whom they could not afford to rebuff. He bombarded both heralds with requests for advice upon ancestral coats of arms for vault bosses, window glass and fabrics. Beckford's infatuation with his medieval descent from Edward III, from Latimers, Mervyns, Seymours, Champernownes, Beauchamps and Bohuns, was another indication of his incurable romanticism. In 1810 he managed to obtain from the College of Heralds by letters patent, not we may be sure without substantial payment, an augmentation to his arms of a 'bordure or, charged with a double tressure flory and counterflory gules', in vindication of his descent, through numerous lines, from the blood royal of Scotland. He had already obtained the right to add the Hamilton crest to his own by a grant of 1798. Genealogy was an obsession with him. As Cyrus Redding his first biographer, remarked: 'It was a singular thing to notice in his conversation the contest between his consciousness of truth and his tendency to favour the obsolete notions of ancestral merit.' At other times his sense of humour got the better of his prejudice and he made huge fun of heraldic pretensions.

All the time that Beckford was at Fonthill Abbey he never had his two daughters to live with him. After the Begum's death in 1798 he put them, still in Lettice's charge, in a separate house in the park. The strange arrangement was not entirely the result of their father's indifference. After the death of Lady Margaret in 1786 a family conclave decided that Beckford was unfit to care for his children, and they were taken away from him. Beckford never forgave his family for the injury done to him. Nevertheless his treatment of the elder daughter Maria Margaret seems to us inexcusably heartless. Samuel Rogers, who remembered her as a child, said she was 'a perfect angel'. She fell in love with a respectable man of good family, Colonel (later Lieut. General) James Orde, one of the Ordes of Weetwood in Northumberland. For some reason Beckford detested him —

Beckford's Swiss dwarf, Perro, who stayed in his master's service forty years.

'one can't trust the least syllable that falls from his porcelainish lips' – and categorically forbade the marriage. Margaret therefore eloped in 1811. Beckford refused to have anything further to do with her. To Franchi, who had evidently told him Margaret was expecting a baby, he wrote in April 1817, 'I don't care who is in the family way . . . if by this somebody you mean Mme Ordure, I spit anew and I curse anew with all my heart – the vilest, lowest animal.' Not a very pretty sentiment. But when later in this same year she lay dying he was apparently reconciled to her. Margaret's daughter, a Mrs. Dunbar, author of *Art and Nature under an Italian Sky*, first published in 1852, proudly referred to herself in 1878 as 'Vathek's granddaughter'.

The younger daughter Susan Euphemia was always his favourite. But then she may have been more pliable. Even so she declined to submit to two suitors whom her father pressed upon her. A Portuguese nobleman of unsuitable habits was one. Thomas Hope of The Deepdene was another Tom Moore noted in his diary that in 1805–6 Hope was making assiduous love to the beautiful Susan Beckford. Hope had in his *Observations* (1804) first raised doubts in Beckford's mind about the propriety of his choice of the Gothic style for Fonthill since every detail of the Abbey compared unfavourably with its equivalent in Salisbury Cathedral. Beckford is said to have acknowledged to Benjamin West that Hope was right. At this date he held Hope in high esteem. But Susan would not accept the ugly little man's proposal of marriage, notwithstanding his large mercantile fortune. Instead she made a far more resplendent match with her stiff-necked cousin Alexander, Marquess of Douglas, afterwards 10th Duke of Hamilton. Beckford's unconcealed delight in this union did not prevent him endeavouring to insert in the marriage contract the conditions that he should be allowed to live with the couple and be given a title. Needless to say the first was rejected out of hand and the second was not in the Marquess's power to bring about. Duke and father-in-law shared the same interests in birth and building, books and collecting. They corresponded regularly and were often together. But it is significant that no one but Beckford was present at the Douglases' wedding and not once did he stay in Hamilton Palace or the London houses which his son-in-law and daughter rented.

By the 1820s Beckford's financial situation was desperate. His debts amounted to £145,000. He was a prey to the three Wildman brothers acting as his solicitor, agent at home and in the West Indies, and banker, who had been battening upon him for decades. He had never bothered the slightest about his Jamaican sugar crops and plantations, some of which he was now losing through Chancery suits to the Wildmans. As an indication of their wealth the eldest son of Thomas Wildman had just bought Newstead Abbey from Byron for 90,000 guineas. Beckford was also beginning to feel his age. He was having trouble with his teeth and his bladder. Fonthill had ceased to be an adventure. It was becoming an

OPPOSITE Susan Euphemia Beckford, Duchess of Hamilton, by Willes Maddox (now at Brodick Castle). Beckford's younger and favourite daughter, and heir to his possessions.

73

anxiety. 'Oh what a fatal abode! Here it smokes, there the wind blows in (and so would the rain if it were raining); every tower is a conveyor of rheumatism,' he complained to Franchi. There was no alternative to getting rid of it.

In 1822 he put the entire Fonthill estate on the market. Christie's compiled and printed a catalogue of the contents of the house, nearly all of which, save a few choice treasures and books, were to go. 72,000 copies of the catalogue were sold at a guinea each. The first day of the sale was announced for 8th October. Excitement among the public was terrific. Dealers, connoisseurs and society ladies flocked to see for themselves the fabulous Caliph's abode of treasure, of which they had heard so many rumours and to which they had never had access. They came from far and wide, and they marvelled. Miss Rushout was one among dozens who recorded their impressions. 'The books were all fixed in their places by one strong brass wire,' she wrote on 16th September in an unpublished journal. She climbed to the top of the tower:

most part of it was very easy, but in some places the stairs were not finished and we were obliged to go up a step-ladder, we passed through one or two rooms that are [yet] to be made habitable . . . It was all very exciting. We saw Mr. Britton employed with his pencil, he had been for two months making drawings and were introduced . . . to the Chev Franchi who gave us permission to drive round the grounds and ordered a Guide to attend us, but we first proceeded on a walk to the American Garden tho on our way we stopt to visit the *Dwarf*, who has a pretty little Garden and a small conservatory, on ringing the bell, we were received with much politeness by the *Genius* of the place who told us he . . . found much amusement in attending to his flowers.

When excitement had reached fever pitch among the eagerly intending bidders a curt notice was posted at the Fonthill gates, two days before the auction was to begin, to the effect that after all estate, house and everything in it had been sold by private treaty. This was the cleverest business deal Beckford ever brought off in his life. The purchaser was in his way almost as eccentric as the vendor. John Farquhar had become a millionaire through selling gunpowder, and was determined to live like a gentleman. At the cost of £330,000 he did, though only for a short time.

Once Fonthill was disposed of Beckford professed to have no regrets, and much relief. 'I am rid of the Holy Sepulchre,' he wrote, 'which no longer interested me since its profanation' by the hordes of sightseers. Nevertheless in spite of the £330,000, more than enough to pay off his debts and mortgages, which he had screwed out of 'old Filthyman', as he called Farquhar, he must have shed some silent tears in parting from the fantastic creation which had made his name famous. Whatever his feelings he had long ago learnt how to put a bold face upon them. The very morning of his departure he summoned his gardener Vincent, and the two of them rode round the garden. As he had done a hundred times before Beckford carefully pointed out to Vincent, who knew as well as he did

Admission ticket to the Fonthill Sale of 1822.

OPPOSITE William Beckford, seated and holding a folio volume. Painted in his middle age by John Hoppner.

Statue of St. Antony of Padua, carved by Joseph Theakston, now in the garden of Wardour Castle.

The present day remains of Fonthill Abbey, showing the Lancaster Tower, Sanctuary and Oratory. Nothing of Beckford's decoration of these apartments has survived.

what was afoot, the alterations and improvements he wanted to make. On returning to the front door of the house he dismounted, and entering his carriage without a word, turned his back on his home for ever.

Less than twelve months later 'old Filthyman' got the auctioneer Phillips to issue another catalogue of the contents of his recently acquired seat, to which Phillips added much indifferent stuff of his own, thus insinuating that it had been Beckford's. At the ensuing sale Beckford managed to buy back a number of his books for less than he got for them.

The sequel to the history of Fonthill calls for a brief relation. In 1825 Beckford was summoned to the deathbed of Wyatt's contractor, who confessed that he had never laid the foundations of the tower according to the specifications for which Beckford had paid him. The tower might, the man warned, fall at any time. Beckford very properly passed on the warning to Farquhar, who made light of it. The tower would last his life, he felt sure, and that was all he cared. He was, as we know, wrong. It fell that very year, at three o'clock in the afternoon of 21st December, destroying the Great Western Hall and the whole of the Octagon, but sparing the organ in the Eastern Vestibule, the galleries and the Great Dining Room. It quietly subsided into the Fountain Court, leaving the west façade unsupported and St. Antony to totter in his niche for at least another twenty years. The Alderman in the Alcove of the Great Western Hall was unharmed, still pointing as it were 'to the ruins of his son's ambitions'. By a miracle no one was injured, although a servant was blown thirty feet down a passage like a pellet through an air gun. Old Filthyman had been wheeled out of the house in his chair when warned of ominous cracking sounds, thought it all nonsense and was wheeled in again. When an hour or so later the tower fell in a cloud of choking dust he heard not a sound. On being informed of what had happened he said he was glad, for now the house would not be too large for him to live in. When Beckford was told, he said the tower had never made obeisance to him, and he wished he had been present to witness how it happened.

The collapse of the tower brought Beckford and Farquhar together. Though the estate was sold just before Farquhar's death, there was talk of his bequeathing Fonthill to his new friend. Beckford was asked if he would have welcomed it. 'Good heavens, yes,' he replied, 'I would have been in an ecstasy, for it would have falsified the proverb, "You can't have your cake and eat it too." '

The estate was split into lots. John Benett of neighbouring Pythouse, M.P. for Wiltshire, bought the Abbey and 400 acres of gardens which were soon bought from him by Lord Grosvenor. By 1835 the Morrison family had acquired the remainder of the estate. Today the Lancaster Tower, the Sanctuary and Oratory are all that is left of what was once the boldest exposition of the Romantic movement in stone, brick and mortar, and possibly the most dramatic country house to have arisen in the English landscape.

6 · LANSDOWN : A FAMOUS LANDMARK

N Monday 22nd September 1817 Beckford had written to Franchi: 'Bath does not please me. After the great spectacle of the Abbey it seems to me incredibly dingy and wretched; and the infamous old men and youths carried in chairs and mechanical carriages round the smoking baths horrify me – a horror not softened by the tender glances of certain old women clad in flounces supremely *à la mode*, who come and go eternally in this paradise of idlers and corpses.'

Yet it was to Bath that Beckford, the moment Fonthill was disposed of, removed his remaining possessions and his not inconsiderable household. The city was at the time in the nadir of its fortunes. Memories of Beau Nash and the cosmopolitan set, of Ralph Allen and the intelligentsia who congregated at Prior Park were faint indeed. Dr. Waagen on a visit about this time saw only one decrepit old lady drawn through the sad streets in a three-wheeled chair. The residents were mostly elderly gentry and retired professional men and their wives, eking out a shallow existence. It was probably on this very account that Beckford decided to take up residence in a social backwater where he was unlikely to meet with competition and rebuffs. For a few months he may have lodged at no. 66 Pulteney Street.

The Bath Chronicle of 2nd July 1823 announced with a splash that

Mr. Beckford is arrived at his house in Lansdown Crescent and engaged in making extensive alterations and arrangements for his unique pictures, books and other rare and costly specimens of art. It is reported that the Gentleman is in treaty for an extensive purchase of land in the rear of the Crescent, with a view to erecting a house in the same. We sincerely hope this is the reason . . . We may anticipate a model of architectural beauty . . .

He had in fact bought from Sir Walter James no. 20, a large house with a rounded central bay at the west end of Lansdown Crescent, which had been built in 1789–92 by a Bath architect, John Palmer, on the extreme northern edge of the city. When Beckford went to live there, open country stretched from his back windows right into the unspoiled Cotswolds. From his front windows he looked in summer down upon a network of grey streets and across the Perpendicular tower of Bath Abbey to the great bulk of Prior Park (which incidentally he would have bought had the price not been too high), its Palladian pavilions straddling Combe Down and reminding him of his lost Splendens. In winter the prospect was obscured by a pall of blue smoke from hundreds of lodging-house chimneys. The situation was high and salutary.

The very first thing he did was to acquire from a certain Ann Lowder the end house of the terrace, then called West Wing, which was separated from Lansdown Crescent by a narrow lane. He connected no. 1 West Wing to the first floor of no. 20 Lansdown Crescent by a bridge. The bridge has three windows under a stone balustrade bearing urns, from which sprout the attenuated leaves of aloes fashioned in grey zinc. Within the bridge a passage (still lined on both sides with oak bookcases just as Beckford had them) used to lead into no. 1 West Wing from a spacious room the width of the house. This room in no. 20 which became his principal library had low bookshelves against the four walls. Over the gilt cornice of the shelves hung portraits by Rembrandt, Bronzino, Titian, Holbein and Velasquez. The heavy window curtains and hangings – for Beckford preferred them to doors between state rooms – were of crimson and deep purple. The Persian carpet was red with a purple fringe. A number of small tables were littered with books. From the high ceiling an ormolu chandelier, now in Kensington Palace, was suspended. For some unknown reason Beckford soon got rid of no. 1 West Wing, which in 1824 assumed the name Lansdown Place West by which it is now known. The Walcot Poor Rate Book for May 1832 gives the owner occupier of no. 1 Lansdown Place West as Admiral Arthur Lysaght. Beckford thereupon filled the far opening of the bridge room with a huge looking glass from floor to ceiling, thus providing one of those long reflected vistas of which he was so fond.

Apart from building the bridge, extensively redecorating rooms. putting up rows of bookcases, moving in books, arranging furniture and

No. 20 Lansdown Crescent, Bath, bought by Beckford in 1823, showing the bridge he built connecting it with No. 1 Lansdown Place West. To the right is No. 19 Lansdown Crescent, acquired in 1837.

hanging pictures, Beckford does not seem to have made structural alterations to no. 20. The front door on the lane opened, as it still opens today, into a generous hall, where the first inanimate object to confront visitors was an impressively framed genealogical tree showing Beckford's descent from Edward III. The first animate object on the other hand was the dwarf. One visitor recorded how on the door bell being answered by an unobtrusive footman, the dwarf was revealed sprawling upon a chair, leering hideously, and doing nothing but pick his nose. A second footman discreetly conducted the visitor up Palmer's original stone staircase with its wrought iron balusters. The walls were hung with family portraits, including Reynolds's full length of the redoubtable Alderman and Romney's of young William leaning haughtily against a classical plinth.

It is interesting to learn from the *Bath Chronicle* report that before he had even settled into his new house Beckford was negotiating for the purchase of land behind the narrow garden of no. 20 on which to build. Build he did, but not, as stated, a house in the rear of the Crescent. The tract of land he bought stretched at least a mile behind the Crescent and at the furthermost end, on the highest point of Lansdown Hill, 800 feet above sea level, Beckford was to raise yet another tower with a few small rooms at its base. It was to be his old age retreat from the world, into which he was to cram many of his most precious works of art. Moreover the fields and downland between the site and the Crescent were to be transformed into an idyllic garden. He was going to follow in the footsteps of his octogenarian great-uncle Charles Hamilton, who fifty years previously had laid out such a garden, only on a smaller scale, behind his house in Royal Crescent. Beckford had as a boy visited the old man in Bath to inspect that urban creation.

He lost no time in obtaining designs for Lansdown Tower from several London and Bath architects. One of the latter was a hitherto unknown architect of twenty-six called Henry Edmund Goodridge, son of a builder-speculator in Bathwick. Goodridge's manner and alertness appealed to him, as did his youth and ductility. He had, too, already built to Beckford's satisfaction the bridge between the two houses. So, rejecting all the established architects' designs, Beckford commissioned Goodridge to start work on the tower in 1825. By the autumn of 1827 the tower, as far as the outside was concerned, was finished. According to the architect's son the work proceeded with lightning rapidity. Within twenty-eight days the block cornice was reached where it was intended to put on the roof. But a belvedere was added after much consultation, again with the intention of taking the roof. 'Mr. Beckford, however, cried, "Higher!" and the lantern was added to crown the summit.' From this account it appears that the tower rose to its 154 feet by a succession of unpremeditated stages. The wonder is that the finished structure became the well proportioned entity it is. Moreover the progress was not without other interruptions. At an early stage the builders, having got wind of the old Powderham scandal,

Lansdown Tower, Bath (1825–7). Drawing by Henry Edmund Goodridge, the Bath architect. The design was closely supervised and certainly dictated by Beckford.

downed tools, insulted Beckford and roundly declared that they would not work for a bugger. Beckford was so incensed that he told Goodridge he would sack the lot, sell up and leave Bath instantly. The situation was only saved by Goodridge's tact and persuasion. These tantrums of Beckford's could be almost uncontrollable. When on a later occasion, he was denied authority to stop a right of way across his new garden, he threatened to sell the whole estate for building plots and go abroad. Again Goodridge found a happy solution by suggesting that a tunnel should be dug under the public footpath.

The style adopted for Lansdown Tower by Beckford was diametrically different from the Anglo-Portuguese Gothic of Fonthill Abbey. David Watkin in his biography of Thomas Hope believes that when dictating the design of Lansdown Tower to Goodridge Beckford, bearing in mind Hope's strictures on Fonthill Abbey, 'repented of his Picturesque extravagance in the Gothic taste and jumped, instead, on the neo-classical band wagon.' Now Beckford seldom repented of anything for long, and there is little reason why he should have repented of what he had done so successfully in the 1790s. Nor was he a man who slavishly followed fashions. Rather he initiated them. It is undeniable that by 1825 he was bored with the Gothic, just as earlier still he had tired of the Palladian. He needed a change. He wanted to experiment with a new style. Indeed Lansdown Tower is in a new style mostly Beckford's own. It has been described variously as Tuscan, Roman, Byzantine and Italo-Greek. Whatever it may be it is not in the straightforward neo-Greek style which early nineteenth-century architects like George Dance had introduced at Stratton Park in 1803–4, John Soane at Dulwich College in 1811–14 or Decimus Burton in the Hyde Park Corner screen the very year when the Lansdown Tower was rising. It makes no use of the orthodox Greek orders, trabeated architraves and depressed pediments. It is something altogether novel.

Drawing by H. E. Goodridge for the library of Lansdown Tower.

There can, I think, be no doubt that David Watkin is substantially correct in his surmise that Beckford was influenced by what Thomas Hope and his architect William Atkinson were doing to The Deepdene near Dorking between 1818 and 1823. But conversely Hope and Atkinson had been influenced by Beckford in that The Deepdene was a late outcrop of the Picturesque harvest of which Fonthill Abbey had been perhaps the earliest, albeit a Gothic one. The Deepdene was an unassimilated conglomeration of styles. It had a curved Greek colonnade on the entrance front and medieval battlements on roofline and turret. It had pointed windows, sash windows and windows with fan heads. It also had two attributes which clearly suggested themselves to the creators of Lansdown Tower, namely an asymmetrical jagged plan, and square Italianate, Palazzo Vecchio-like tower of the sort which throughout Queen Victoria's reign was to be frequently reproduced on suburban villas. The irregular plan and square tower common to both buildings were essentially Picturesque, and intended to accord with the naturalistic gardens in which both were set. But the tower feature of the Lansdown complex – which is of course infinitely smaller in scale than was The Deepdene house – is stylistically less eclectic than idiosyncratic. It is not Revivalist. It is sheer nineteenth-century as opposed to eighteenth-century Beckfordian.

The virtue of the Picturesque plan, which The Deepdene and the Lansdown Tower exemplify, is that additions can judiciously be made to it without unduly detracting from the balance of the whole. Seen from the south, Lansdown Tower is built up in three recessive stages: a single-storey block, originally comprising bedroom, kitchen and pump room; next a two-storey block, nearly square, containing a suite of elegant little rooms in which Beckford housed his treasures. On the east side of the parapet a pair of chimney stacks, united by an arch, points like an apostrophe to the third stage. This is the base of the great tower, the smooth and windowless south front of which rides against the open sky.

Choragic monument of Lysicrates, at Athens: a plate from Stuart and Revett, *Antiquities of Athens* (1762). The prototype of many English park follies and of the lantern on Lansdown Tower.

Above the projecting block cornice is the 'Belvidere', as Goodridge spelt it. It has on each face three tall vertical windows with arches inside square-headed openings. The windows are glazed with sheets of plate glass, an innovation with which Beckford was inordinately pleased, so much so that he removed the sash bars from his Lansdown Crescent houses and substituted plate glass. Certainly the Belvedere windows give the illusion of being unglazed and provide wonderfully uninterrupted views to north, south, east and west. On clear days Beckford would trip up the carpeted treads of the twisted staircase and sit on an X-shaped stool, with nothing between him and the hills of Wales, the silver strip of Bristol Channel, the blue Wiltshire downs or the limitless horizons of the Cotswolds according to the direction he chose to survey. Indeed were it not for the outside cross-rail up to knee level these windows which reach practically from floor to ceiling would be horribly vertiginous. In Beckford's time thick crimson curtains could be drawn on a circular rod to keep out the sun in summer. In winter wafts of warm air rose from a tall urn of polished granite and bronze at the foot of the staircase. The Belvedere ceiling which largely survives, is a shallow saucer dome of recessed panels resting on a deep cornice with honeysuckle frieze all in stucco.

Above the Belvedere the crowning feature of the tower is the lantern, a recognizable adaptation of the Choragic monument of Lysicrates in Athens although different from the prototype in every detail. Whereas the original is circular on a square plinth, the Lansdown version is octagonal on a polygonal plinth, with urns at each corner. The columns of the lantern and the parapet of the plinth are of cast iron. Beckford had the cupola and finial gilded, and when dusk crept across the high plateau and up the tower, the beacon could still be seen from miles away brilliantly reflecting the last rays of the setting sun.

Unfortunately no architectural drawings of Lansdown Tower beyond two views by Goodridge have survived from which we can deduce whether client or architect was responsible for the overall design of the tower outside and in. But our surmise is that since Beckford was a man of long experience with very positive tastes, and Goodridge was young and comparatively inexperienced, the inspiration came from the former and the particular details were worked out by the latter. Fortunately we have the handsome folio volume on Lansdown Tower published just after Beckford's death in 1844. The text by E. F. English, auctioneer, dealer and purveyor of furnishings in Milsom Street, Bath, had been closely supervised by Beckford. The richly coloured plates drawn by Willes Maddox, a young local artist from whom Beckford commissioned three paintings of New Testament scenes for the lunettes of the sanctuary, were submitted for his approval. The book describes and the plates illustrate the tower as it was furnished at the very end of Beckford's life, for in 1841 he had sold through English's auction rooms several paintings and much

The top of Lansdown
Tower, Bath.

The Crimson Drawing Room in
Lansdown Tower as it was at
the very end of Beckford's life,
from Willes Maddox's plate in
Views of Lansdown Tower (1844).

furniture from the tower. English stated that this was done 'with the view
of refurnishing the whole more classically, as it now stands.' In other
words Beckford may have got rid of eighteenth-century objects of high
quality in favour of those several pieces, ebony cabinets and stools, coin
cabinets with little drawers, chiffoniers, coffers and sideboards of yellow
varnished oak, which he deemed more suitable to the architecture of the
tower, and which are so conspicuously displayed in Maddox's plates.
These extraordinary objects (of which one cabinet was practically a
replica of the arched chimney stack of the kitchen wing) are sufficiently
distinctive as to be, surely, the products of Beckford's invention and
Goodridge's expertise, for an old friend stated after Beckford's death that
he had designed nearly every piece of his new furniture. Of inferior design
and quality to Hope's Empire style sofas, chairs and tables of veneered
mahoganies in the Egyptian and Greek tastes, Beckford's new furniture
anticipated the solid, rather coarse stuff which we associate generically
with mid-Victorian lodging houses.

The general impression of the rooms was one of great opulence. Doors with narrow plate glass panels and large circular headed mirrors, helped by through-views and reflections to suggest that the dimensions of the drawing rooms, libraries and vestibule were less restricted than in fact they were. The ceilings were wainscoted, beams and recessed panels painted purple and crimson, and cornices gilded. Fireplaces were of Brocatelle marbles; curtains of either plain purple velvet or crimson silk. The windows, which are all small and round headed, then had double diamond panes of which the leads were gilded internally so as to give 'an appearance of perpetual sunshine'. Those people who were privileged to visit the tower, Dr. Waagen, Cyrus Redding, Mr. Lansdown, E. F. English and others, all praised the flawless taste with which pictures, porcelain, maiolica, books, bronzes, Etruscan urns, Japanese vases, enamelled and jewelled cups, silver-gilt salts and gold mounted nautilus shells were displayed. What especially pleased Dr. Waagen was 'that all these things bear a due proportion in size to the moderate apartments in which they are, and are likewise so arranged that they serve richly to adorn each other, without producing, as so often happens, by overloading and confusion, the disagreeable effect of auction rooms.'

Lansdown Tower was the first building of importance on which H. E. Goodridge was engaged. The young protégé was soon launched on a number of Bath projects along the Italo-Greek Picturesque lines which were Beckford's second contribution to English architecture. This is not the place to investigate Goodridge's remarkable villas on Bathwick Hill, the names of which, Montebello, Casa Bianca, La Casetta and Fiesole, vociferously proclaim the Tuscan element imparted to his architecture by his patron. For Beckford had learnt from Uvedale Price 'how little the buildings [of Bath] are made to yield to the ground, and how few trees are

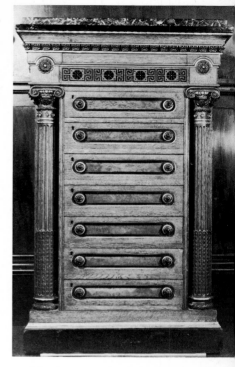

Medal Cabinet in oak inlaid with ebony, and parcel gilt, formerly in Lansdown Tower.

Ornamental furniture, designed by Beckford and Goodridge for Lansdown Tower, from a plate by Willes Maddox in E. F. English's *Lansdown Tower* (1844).

85

mixed with them' and he awakened Goodridge to the fact that the hills surrounding the city resembled Italian landscape and called for the same architectural treatment as the foothills of Fiesole and the other suburbs of Florence – a fact which struck Walter Savage Landor when he called Bath 'England's Florence'.

Although Goodridge was deeply involved in the later 1820s and the 1830s in other projects – the essentially neo-Greek Cleveland Bridge across The Avon and the great perron at Prior Park among them – he remained closely associated with Beckford until the Caliph's death. He was one of the few residents of Bath to be regularly received at Lansdown Crescent, sharing not only his client's interests in architecture, but in works of art and literature too. However, although he made subsequent alterations to Beckford's Lansdown Crescent houses, the tower was his pride and joy. It is specifically mentioned on his tombstone. His concern for it exceeded Beckford's. When in the 1840s Goodridge learnt that the tower had been broken into by vandals (although nothing was stolen), he rushed in a frenzy of anxiety to Lansdown Crescent. He found Beckford unconcernedly throwing bread to his turkeys in the garden. 'Mr. Goodridge, Mr. Goodridge,' the old man exclaimed, 'don't be so excited! Don't show such emotion! Where will you and I and the tower be in a few years?' It was like Beckford to belittle such enthusiasm. He once dismissed a friend's praise of the tower with the comment 'Such as it is, it is a famous landmark for the drunken farmers on their return from market.'

Goodridge also collaborated with Beckford in the layout of the grounds behind Lansdown Crescent. The tower was of course the pole star, the distant focal point of the grounds. It was exactly one mile from the

Objects of Vertu, No. 1. A plate by W. Maddox showing some of Beckford's treasures kept in Lansdown Tower.

Bloodstone bowl with setting by Paul Storr, now in the Barber Institute collection. It can be seen in centre of previous plate.

Crescent. Beckford knew before he moved into no. 20 that the circumscribed town garden at the rear of the house, separated from the lane by a grey stone wall over which fruit trees thickly clustered, could never satisfy him after Fonthill's limitless domain. So he busily bought up the separate farms and fields on the rising ground and the windswept plateau as far as the site of the tower. He began by extending the existing garden of no. 20 into the quarry a little to the west of his stables. He levelled the ground, in the middle of which he excavated a pool approached by a broad path spread with glistening quartz. On either side he put mixed flower and vegetable beds. He cut sloping terraces into the steep cliff of the quarry. On the highest terrace he raised a gateway to mark the boundary of the enclosed garden. Embattled and machicolated, with rounded arch and iron-studded door beneath a spurious coat of arms, which Beckford had incidentally no right to bear, the engaging structure is neither neo-Greek nor neo-Italian, but neo-Norman, a mild foreflavour of what Thomas Hopper was about to produce on an immense scale at Penrhyn Castle. From the stables a bridle-path between high walls met the garden path at this point. As though to prove that no architectural style

87

The Embattled Gateway, behind the garden of the Lansdown Crescent houses.

was beyond his eclecticism Beckford built a minute Moorish summer house with Saracenic opening, onion dome and crescent. Beckford admitted to Mr. Lansdown that he did not much care for the Moorish taste, and there are few instances of his having indulged it. The exquisite agate and chalcedony cup has a stem and cover mounted by the silversmith Joseph Angell in 1815–16, in Saracenic pattern, surely dictated by Beckford.

Once through the Embattled Gateway the narrow, mile long landscape was wholly different from the tamed garden within the walled precincts. Mr. English's somewhat stilted phraseology gives a fair idea of what it looked like. 'The first part of the way to the tower,' he wrote, 'on the slope of Lansdown Hill appears, offering an easy ascent.' Thenceforward the walk was uninterrupted.

Diversified by plantations and studded with cottages in the Italian taste, the grounds, the whole way, present scenery artfully blended into one harmonious whole. Yet, although the resources of art are put in abundant requisition, there is no trace of cultivation – nothing either park-like or formal – all is kept, as much as possible, in subjugation to the modesty of Nature.

In other words Beckford had trodden the Picturesque path even further into the open wilderness than he had done at Fonthill, where within the Barrier the grounds, with their long intersecting rides and distinctive American and Alpine sections, could not be mistaken for anything but a gentleman's conscious parkscape. Here the ultimate attempt at naturalism was achieved. The unwary visitor might be deceived into supposing that he was traversing a totally virginal landscape. Only the wary would appreciate that it was nature firmly under control.

English went on to explain why Beckford became so enamoured of the spot. It was because

the vicinity of Bath has, unquestionably, more of the southern cast of character than that of any other English city. Those to whom the neighbourhood of Rome is familiar [in contradistinction to Florence it now appears] have spoken of a certain resemblance that the boundary to which we are alluding carries in common with the Campagna di Roma.

One evening the writer, accompanying Mr. Beckford through the grounds, after a visit to the Tower, was curious to learn what reconciled him so perfectly to the locality of Lansdown after the vastness of Fonthill, with its extensive gardens and groves of almost Oriental beauty. In putting the question it was felt with what courtesy and candour it would be answered. Extending his arms and elevating his voice, as if excited by 'the poet's fire,' he exclaimed, '*This!* – This! – the finest prospect in Europe!' pointing to the vast panoramic view around, to the countless hills near, the far Welsh mountains, the blue fading distance, and then to the most beautiful of our ancient cities, which at that moment slept beneath, enveloped in the rich purple mist of a summer sunset, – 'This!' he repeated.

Mr. Lansdown, a more discerning visitor than the enthusiastic auctioneer of Milsom Street, believed that Beckford had in mind Claude's landscapes of long, distant horizontal hills punctuated by vertical towers in the foreground and sprinkled with humble peasants' cottages in the middle

Moorish summer house built by Beckford at the back of his garden at No. 20 Lansdown Crescent.

Vignette in Rutter's *Delineations of Fonthill* (1823). The agate cup (shown on opposite page) can be seen on the left of the group.

One of six silver-gilt plates matching the cup (opposite page). Beckford went on collecting until the year of his death, 1844.

An agate and chalcedony cup,
of which the cover and stem
were mounted by Joseph
Angell, 1815–16, in Saracenic
pattern. Now in the Victoria
and Albert Museum.

William Beckford on horseback, in old age. A lithograph by John Doyle.

distance. After seeing Lansdown Tower he exclaimed, 'Who but a man of extraordinary genius would have thought of rearing in the desert such a structure as this, or creating such an oasis?' Indeed within an incredibly short time the barren, inhospitable and exposed down was miraculously transformed. The 'naturalness' was most cunningly brought about. Not only was an Italianate villa with an archway over the path fashioned out of a farm building, a 'yawning cavern' out of a quarry, a subterranean grotto out of beetling cliffs, and water made to drip into a goldfish pond from rocks, but trees, shrubs and plants were introduced from all parts of the world.

Beckford was extremely fortunate in his head gardener, the incomparable Vincent, successor to one Milne, who occupied the post when Loudon first visited Fonthill in 1807 and supplied William Cobbett in 1811 with fir cones and seeds. Beckford had not cared for Milne but was

92

devoted to Vincent, who remained in his service for fifty years and was a mourner at his funeral. Outspoken yet respectful, Vincent was about the only member of Beckford's household or even family who dared address him with complete freedom. To Beckford's question on one occasion, 'Do you think me a fool, Vincent?' the gardener was overheard to reply, 'Yes, your honour.' Vincent was not only knowledgeable but capable. Nothing was an obstacle to him. Nothing was too much trouble. 'If you find the money, sir, I will find the trees,' he said. Accordingly Vincent planted close to the tower conifers of every species, Italian, Brazilian, Mexican, Siberian and Scotch; Irish yews, a fir from Larissa, another from a high peak of the Himalayas, maples from America, a rose tree brought specially from Pekin. From Fonthill he carted fully grown apple trees — they bore no fruit but 'they blossom in the spring and look pretty, and that is all master cares about' — lavender, rosemary, marjoram and heliotrope. Between them Beckford and Vincent did indeed create an oasis in a desert.

Every morning of the year until a few weeks before his death, unless the wind was in the east when nothing normally induced him to set foot outside the house, Beckford, after drinking a cup of chicken broth, would ride early to the tower. He was attended by a cavalcade, preceded by a grey-haired old steward on horseback, then two grooms with long hunting whips. Next rode Beckford with five or six dogs, and in the rear two more grooms with whips. The stamping and clattering of hooves was enough to rouse all the neighbours in the Crescent from their matutinal slumbers. But how much did Beckford care? Not a jot. As soon as he reached the tower he would throw his horse's reins to a groom and rapidly climb to the Belvedere to admire the panorama. He would then wander through the rooms, arrange a bouquet of flowers in a bowl as carefully as if he were painting a still-life, pull out a book from the shelves, read a passage or two, re-arrange the furniture and walk home to breakfast, the cattle in the fields trotting up to him as he passed and nuzzling his elbow for titbits. To the end of his life his love of animals and their love for him were a source of general amazement. Birds were said to sing for him when they were dumb to others. And he certainly did everything to encourage them by allowing dense thickets and brambles to grow close to the tower, which became a haunt of nightingales.

Today not a vestige of Beckford's landscaped grounds survives if we except a short strip from his stables to the Embattled Gateway. The derelict site of the kitchen garden has been bought for development. Schools and blocks of flats now stand on the pastures and the Tower garden is again a field. Even at this time of writing Beckford's Plantation is being clear felled. Only a row of lime trees which he planted along Lansdown road for the enjoyment of an undeserving public has been suffered to remain.

> groves of Eden, vanish'd now so long
> Live in description, and look green in song.

7 · BATH : LANSDOWN CRESCENT

LTHOUGH Beckford's life after 1823 was uneventful and fairly solitary, it was not by any means empty. Once Lansdown Tower was completed in 1828 his creative activities were nearing their end. It is true he continued to titivate the interior of the tower but only to the extent of rearranging pictures and furniture. It is also true that he was tinkering with Lansdown Crescent even in the 1830s. No. 1 Lansdown Place West having been disposed of he turned about, so to speak, and looked in the opposite direction. He bought and altered the adjacent house to no. 20 on the east side, namely no. 19. And he resumed his writing in so far as he refurbished and published some of the journals of his youth. But these efforts can hardly be described as major works of invention. In fact he devoted the greater surplus of his energies to collecting. He had begun collecting in extreme youth, and he continued into extreme old age.

The astonishing thing about Beckford as collector was the catholicity of his interest in works of art. There were no limits to the variety, style or date of the objects which took his fancy and had to be acquired, whether missals, psalters, miniatures, bronzes, jade, Venetian glasses, *tazzas*, or porcelain. It would be tedious to relate where many of these possessions have been re-housed today. In 1818 he bought for £450 the so-called Rubens vase, a fourth/fifth-century Romano-Byzantine object cut from a single agate; in 1819 for £285 the Hungarian topaz vase, rich in gold, diamonds and enamel, said by some to have been made for the marriage of Catherine Cornaro to the King of Cyprus in 1472, and by others attributed to Cellini. During his visit to the Portuguese monastery of Alcobaça in 1794, Beckford coveted a Gothic reliquary, 'the model of a cathedral in the style of the Sainte Chapelle at Paris . . . Ten times at least did I examine and almost worship this highly wrought precious specimen of early art.' Did it resemble the central reliquary depicted in Van der Weyden's *Exhumation of St. Hubert* (now in the National Gallery) which he bought at a later date? We do not know. But we do know from illustrations that the exquisite late twelfth-century Limoges enamelled reliquary, which became one of his greatest treasures, closely resembled that on the altar in St. Hubert's picture.

As patron and collector of contemporary paintings Beckford was immensely discerning. When a mere boy he invited Loutherbourg to paint landscape murals at Splendens. When at the age of twenty-one he contemplated publishing his first book of travels, he commissioned G-B Cipriani to illustrate it. He was taught drawing (at which he did not excel) by Alexander Cozens, and took with him on a European tour his son J. R. Cozens. The younger Cozens was the first British artist to paint water-

OPPOSITE *The Exhumation of St. Hubert*, attributed to Van der Weyden, formerly in Beckford's possession, now in the National Gallery.

One of a pair of silver-gilt vases with ivory 'sleeves' carved in the Low Countries, perhaps by François Langhemans, *c.* 1700. London hallmarks, 1811. Maker's mark: David Willaume. Owned by Beckford, formerly in collection of Lady Betty Germaine (died 1769), the Margravine of Anspach (Wilding Bequest).

Watercolour of Lake Nemi by
J. R. Cozens, now the property of
the National Trust at Stourhead,
Wilts. Cozens toured Italy
under Beckford's patronage.

colours in Italy, and in John Constable's view the greatest genius among English landscape painters. At the age of twenty-three Beckford received a letter from [A.C.H.] Vernet, saying, 'I would prefer to work for you than for any other person because if I am fortunate enough to produce something good, you will perceive it. I only wish I could express the impression that you have made on me.' The sale catalogue of pictures compiled after Beckford's death discloses that he had at different times acquired a hundred sketches by Bonington. A bound album contained twenty-six drawings by Prout, Copley Fielding, Shotter Boys, and the Daniells. He possessed, and sold in his lifetime ninety-five watercolours by J. R. Cozens and paintings by Girtin, Ibbetson, Etty, Landseer, Stothard and Nasmyth. He was an enthusiastic admirer of Blake's engraved and hand-illuminated books, some of which he bought, having been one of the few persons to attend an exhibition of Blake's drawings in 1809. Other contemporary artists whose paintings he possessed were Warwick Smith (156 views), Cattermole, de Cort (18 views), John Coney (35 pencil drawings of buildings), Charles Wild, H. F. Worsley, G. Barrett jnr., Pether, the younger Crome, Gainsborough, Richard Wilson, James Ward and Samuel Palmer. It is an impressive list.

Beckford's choice of Old Masters was catholic and advanced. He bought pictures because they pleased him, not because they belonged to a particular school. He never haggled with dealers or owners. He stated his price, which was rejected or accepted, usually the latter. He professed to look four or five times at a picture, and once having made up his mind did not change it. He seldom made a mistake. One of his regrets was that he could not afford to buy Sir Thomas Lawrence's incomparable collection of Old Master drawings. But at least he had the discernment soundly to trounce the philistinism of the British government for not buying them for the nation. He developed the experienced connoisseur's keen eye for detection of fakes and was highly suspicious of restored paintings. On the whole he did not care for Flemish paintings, although he admired the landscapes of Berghems and Wouvermans. He was repelled by Rubens. He confessed to being bored by Tintoretto and Veronese. By contrast he was among the first Englishmen to appreciate and buy Italian Primitives; and he greatly admired Giovanni Bellini whom his contemporaries, and even successors like Eastlake, despised. The National Gallery contains at least twenty Old Masters formerly in his ownership. At Hampton Court, in the London Museum, the Berlin Museum, the Metropolitan and Frick Museums,

Crucifixion, in the style of Orcagna, formerly owned by Beckford, now the property of the National Gallery. There are twenty of Beckford's pictures in the National Gallery.

97

and the Thyssen collection several of Beckford's pictures are hanging today.

Of all those persons who at different times were privileged to see Beckford's collections, the two most qualified to judge them were the critic William Hazlitt and the German art historian Dr. G. F. Waagen. Neither met Beckford. The Englishman dismissed the collections as 'affectedly mean, elaborately little and ostentatiously perverse. What shall we say to a collection,' this respected critic declaimed, 'which uniformly and deliberately rejects every great work, and every great name in art, to make room for idle rarities and curiosities of mechanical skill?' Yet the author of *Vathek*, he conceded, was not himself a *petit-maître*. Oh dear no! 'His genius as a writer "hath a devil." ' Is it possible that the clear-headed Hazlitt was confusing his artistic with his moral judgement?

Just before Beckford acquired no. 19 Lansdown Crescent the distinguished Dr. Waagen paid a visit to Bath. This was in early September of 1835. On arrival at his hotel he immediately despatched a note to Beckford begging to be allowed to see his art treasures. The messenger came back with the note unopened and the advice that, since Beckford never received letters from strangers, he should make application to the steward. On this being done permission was readily given. Waagen went to Lansdown Tower and Lansdown Crescent without however meeting his host at either place. Although the tickets granted him a two-hour visit to both tower and house the doctor was so hustled around by ignorant and disobliging housekeepers that he was unable to inspect the treasures as thoroughly as he would have liked. The housekeeper in the Crescent even refused to pull back the curtains to enable him to examine the pictures closely. Nevertheless he was dazzled by the display of gems, cameos, maiolica, treasures of all sorts, and above all paintings. He made a list of the principal pictures and other contents in each room, which is published in *Works of Art and Artists in England*, vol. 3 (1838). Of all the rooms he entered the front dining-room on the ground floor of no. 20 impressed him most.

I shall never forget the dining-room, which taken all in all, is perhaps one of the most beautiful in the world. Conceive a moderate apartment of agreeable proportions, whose walls are adorned with cabinet pictures, the noblest productions of Italian art of the time of Raphael, from the windows of which you overlook the whole paradisaical valley of the Avon, with the city of Bath, which was now steeped in sunshine. Conceive in it a company of men of genius and talent, between the number of the Graces and Muses, whose spirits are duly raised by the choicest viands, in the preparation of which the refined culinary art of our days has displayed its utmost skill, by a selection of wines, such as nature and human care produce only on the most favoured spots of the earth, in the most favourable years, and you will agree with me that many things here meet in a culminating point, which, even singly, are calculated to rejoice the heart of man.

Of all the pictures he pored over, Raphael's *St. Catherine*, Garofolo's *Holy Family* and Elsheimer's exquisite *Little Tobias* seem to have pleased him

Claude, *Arrival of Aeneas at Pallanteum*. Anglesey Abbey.

most. He 'came away with the conviction that Mr. Beckford unites, in a very rare degree, an immense fortune with a general and refined love of art and a highly cultivated taste.' Waagen at any rate recognized that whatever else Beckford may have been, he was a prince of aesthetes.

It is gratifying to learn that although Beckford did not see fit to meet his distinguished guest he entertained him so hospitably. It was a habit he had, to lavish every luxury upon important people under his roof while withholding his society if he suspected that they had ulterior motives of some sort, curiosity, impertinence or even display of superior knowledge to his own. He entertained the Duchess of Gordon at Fonthill for a week without once making an appearance, because he knew she had an eye to marrying one of her daughters to him; and on another occasion having invited several M.P.s to dinner he did not join them because he feared

100

they might snub him. He had not forgotten how his neighbour Sir Richard Colt Hoare of Stourhead, after dining with him, had been warned by the local magistrates that if ever he accepted a second invitation to Fonthill he would be ostracized.

Whereas throughout the Bath years Beckford continued to buy pictures, he also sold those he grew tired of – not, let it be said at once, without financial profit, for he had considerable business acumen. As long ago as 1808 he had got rid of the Altieri Claudes for 12,000 guineas having bought them in 1799 for 6,500. His chief reason was that Claude had become a too popular artist for a person of his esoteric tastes. He sold to the National Gallery Garofolo's *Holy Family* and Mazzolino's *Trinity with the Madonna*, the last for 1,000 guineas which was more than double what he paid for it; also Raphael's famous *St. Catherine* for 6,000 guineas, having paid 2,000 for it, and Perugino's scarcely less famous *Virgin and Child with St. John* at an equally satisfactory profit. As late as 1844 he sold to the National Gallery for 600 guineas Bellini's *Doge Loredan*, which had cost him only 300. But his reason for disposing of these pictures was not merely financial. Everyone who saw them, including Dr. Waagen, raved about them, and overpraise of the obvious was enough to turn Beckford against it. His taste in pictures became more and more selective as he grew older. He has already been referred to as one of the earliest connoisseurs to appreciate Italian Primitives: he even anticipated William Roscoe, the Liverpool merchant, and W. Y. Ottley, Keeper of Prints and Drawings at the British Museum, in this specialized pursuit. Their attraction to Primitive paintings was more academic than genuinely art loving. Only the Earl of Bristol, Bishop of Derry, bought paintings by Cimabue and Giotto before Beckford's time. This remarkable prelate's enlightened approach to pictures was, like Beckford's, totally disinterested and unaffected.

Beckford's taste in schools of painting was certainly eclectic, as we know from the wide assortment of pictures that found a way to his collections over the years. His chief preference was for the Italian. His recorded comments to visitors privileged to see his pictures show that his judgements were based upon an understanding of the moods, motives and ideals of the artists who had painted them. Like most men of his generation he looked for a message, if not a moral in a picture. He believed that to find it the connoisseur must first steep himself in the period to which the picture belonged. He said to Cyrus Redding:

One must become half-Catholic to enter fully into the glories of Italian art – religion with us is a cold, reluctant duty. We acknowledge God, but fear to love him. We are afraid of anything that fits our minds for devotion – we make religion a duty, not an affection – when the formality of worship is over, we have done. The true spirit, superstition, devotion, whatever you will – was in the heart of the Italian artist – it oozed out at the end of his pencil, bathing his work in the beauty of holiness.

Doge Leonardo Loredan by Giovanni Bellini, formerly owned by Beckford, now the property of the National Gallery.

LEFT No. 19 Lansdown Crescent, Bath. The perspective staircase altered for Beckford, presumably by Goodridge *c.* 1837. He called the lobby shrouded by a crimson silk blind, 'The Hall of Eblis'.

RIGHT View through the window of Beckford's library in Lansdown Crescent.

This was an extraordinarily objective and well considered remark, as well as a bold one, for an Englishman to make during the first half of the nineteenth century. It could only have come from a cosmopolitan Englishman, who besides having a consuming love of pictures, had lived among Latin artists long enough to investigate and admire the forces which impelled them towards their chosen fields of expression. No wonder then that he developed with the years the astute collector's uncanny flair for a good painting, one which cannot be passed on to another unless he is prepared to go the hard way to achieve it. Having advised Franchi on one occasion to look, and look again, he wrote, 'For drawings you must have a sure nose, extremely sure.'

So great was Beckford's reverence for good paintings that he was made furious by their unskilled restoration and over-painting by what he called 'scavengers'. Boyd Alexander quotes his indignant comments on Titian's *Martyrdom of St. Peter* when he saw it at the Louvre after Napoleon had looted it from Venice, as 'almost covered with a glare of false colours' by French restorers, and Raphael's *Transfiguration* 'patched like a sea captain's cassock at the end of a voyage round the world'. He also strongly deprecated pictures being transferred from panel to canvas and touched up in the process.

The first mention in the Walcot rate book of Beckford being owner

occupier of no. 19 Lansdown Crescent comes under March 1837. Up to that year the house was entered under the name of Irwin. 'Now had I not bought this house,' Beckford told Redding, 'I would have been perpetually annoyed by the ticking of some cursed jack, the jingling of some beastly piano, horrid-toned bells tinkling, and so on. The only way to avoid this was by buying the house; and so I bought it, to the infinite annoyance and astonishment of the Bath aristocracy, an odd breed, I believe.' There is reason for supposing that at first Beckford did not intend to use it, but to keep it empty. Mr. Irwin had died in 1831 and presumably his widow followed him four or five years later. But the temptation to spread himself was too much for Beckford. Goodridge was called in and straightway began to make alterations. When Mr. Lansdown was introduced by Goodridge to Lansdown Crescent in 1838 he described no. 19 as 'recently fitted up'. Doorways were made in the party wall between the two houses and through views contrived from one to the other, ending in mirrors. Palmer's conventional stair balusters were removed from no. 19, as was the stairwell. In their place a tunnel-like staircase was substituted, with at intervals strips or belts running from the dado across a barrel vault. Beckford professed that his reason for the curious arrangement was to exclude draughts. It may have been that he disliked being spied upon by his servants. From the entrance passage, lit only by the front door fanlight

The 'Grecian Library' in No. 19, with scagliola pilasters between mahogany bookcases, made c. 1837.

103

Some of Beckford's rare books. He amassed throughout his life old books and precious bindings, and had modern books rebound by the best contemporary binders. From Sotheby's Sale Catalogue, 4th July 1966.

over which a crimson silk blind was stretched, the staircase looked like a row of arches in perspective. Because of the gloom engendered Beckford jokingly called the passage, as he had once seriously named the Egyptian Hall of Splendens, the Hall of Eblis. His chief innovation however was the making of another library to run parallel with the entrance passage. This handsome room, its three inner walls divided by yellow scagliola pilasters carrying arched recesses, in which Beckford put Etruscan urns, has bookcases of red figured mahogany. The library in no. 19 is the only room (apart from the bridge passage leading from no. 20) in all Beckford's houses to survive as he knew and used it. 'The room in which I study,' he told Redding, 'is that . . . which you most properly call a Grecian library, for so it is.'

In a letter to *The Times* of 19th January 1882 Henry G. Bohn, who in 1834 became Beckford's bookseller, described him as 'the greatest book enthusiast I ever knew, who preferred Aldines and other early books bearing insignia of such as Francis I, Henri et Diane [de Poitiers] and de Thou, and especially choice old morocco bindings by Dessueil, Pasdeloup, and Derome.' Certainly Beckford's bibliophilic interests began early. Soon after coming of age he acquired part of Edward Wortley Montagu's collection of oriental manuscripts. In 1783 he bought rare books and illuminated manuscripts at the Croft sale. In 1784 he bought more rare manuscripts at the Duc de la Vallière's sale in Paris, and valuable books besides, outbidding the King of France and the Holy Roman Emperor. In 1791–2 he was frenziedly salvaging choice volumes from the libraries of the French aristocrats which were being broken up. Until he left Fonthill Beckford did not hesitate to put on the market those of his books for which he had no further use. Notwithstanding frequent sales by him his collection continued to multiply. By the time of the sale of Fonthill Abbey in 1822, apart from the books his library also contained 800 illuminated manuscripts ranging from the ninth to the sixteenth century. Beckford bought back hundreds of books the following year (characteristically for less than he sold them for), and during the remainder of his life amassed more selectively what proved to be one of the greatest collections of all time. Practically until the day of his death he went on buying books. His methods were canny. He looked cautiously on sales, such as the Duke of Roxburghe's in 1812, at which record prices were expected. He bided his time. When the Duke of Marlborough went suddenly bankrupt in 1819 he picked up many a bargain. He was able to snatch up a valuable Froissart for £32 at a moment when the Persian Ambassador in his exotic robes passed the auctioneer's premises and the majority of competitors rushed to the window to look at him.

Books were here, there and everywhere throughout both houses, ranged on shelves, piled on tables and stacked on the floor, seemingly in no order. Yet Beckford knew precisely where an individual volume was, and would flit across the room and pounce upon it accurately like a bird of prey. If by some mischance it had been shifted by a servant dusting there was hell for the housekeeper to pay. Were Beckford looking for an excuse for extending his premises, it certainly could have been to accommodate his ever increasing library. During the Bath period Beckford's book acquisitiveness was intensified. He never forgot his folly and consequent misery in having parted with thousands of books to Farquhar in 1822. Nor did he ever part with a book again.

It goes without saying that Beckford preferred special editions, printed on the finest paper, and when they were old, bound in the finest morocco, for he was the most selective of bibliophiles. Yet he seldom, if ever, bought a book which he did not read. He was an omnivorous reader. John Britton attested that his faculty for reading was extraordinary. He would finish a good sized octavo volume during his breakfast. 'He caught a sentence at a look; he did not recognize and dwell on a word, but embraced the whole at a glance.' He was blessed with a most retentive memory. He was a fairly faithful patron of booksellers until they either died, went out of business or greatly displeased him. He rated them at one moment, and lauded them the next. His first English bookseller was Theophilus Thornton who set up in London in 1784, and died young in 1796. In Paris Auguste Chardin was his bookseller and the friend who protected him during the Terror. Chardin introduced him to the famous binder N. D. Derome le jeune. George Clarke and his son William of New Bond Street were his booksellers until the death of the latter in 1830. William was nicknamed by his patron 'Boletus', the Latin for mushroom, which his large head and short body resembled.

The Clarkes were succeeded by Henry G. Bohn, who on Beckford's death valued the library for the Duke of Hamilton at £30,000. But the Duchess would not have her father's books sold. When however her grandson included them in the Sotheby's Hamilton Palace sale of 1882–3 Bohn again catalogued and arranged them. They fetched the prodigious total of £73,551. 18s. Bohn declared that when Beckford was in London during the season he had visited his shop almost daily.

Beckford's first bookbinder from 1787 until 1804, when he went broke, was a German immigrant, Christian Samuel Kalthoeber. He specialized in red or blue morocco, calf or russia bindings. Until 1815 Beckford employed no exclusive binder. In that year he came upon Charles Smith, who although referred to by his client as 'Beast Smith' served him on and off until 1831. But for ten years until death removed him in 1836 the favourite binder was Charles Lewis. He was the son of a German immigrant and moved to Duke Street, St. James's in 1817. Lewis, the 'Angel', was in such demand by other clients that he often had to turn down Beckford's orders, greatly to the Caliph's indignation. His bindings were usually simple, sometimes distinguished by the tooled emblems of the Latimer cross and Hamilton cinquefoil. Beckford described Lewis at a moment when the bookbinder was in high esteem as 'the first artist in this line that Europe can boast of. His works alone are worthy to range in the Tower of Lansdown with the Pasdeloup, de Soeil, de Rome, etc.' Another binder was the much abused John Wilson – 'Beast Wilson, who would have been long since at the Regent Park Zoological were I empowered to make out the mandamus.'

Beckford did not leave it to these craftsmen to choose the bindings for his books. He had his own ideas and his directions were explicit. Here is a typical one for Bunyan's *Pilgrim's Progress*: 'Let it be bound in some choice little scrap of genuine rough-grained blue morocco – accent of the last *e* correct and accurate – inside, red within a border of blue morocco, said border with blind tooled fillets somewhat antiquated.'

Beckford's books were looked after with scrupulous attention according to a report in *The Times* of 18th July 1822. They were always protected from the direct sunlight. No gas was permitted in his libraries. Nor were these rooms lit by oil lamps or entered after dark. The bookcases were not glazed or closed in any way that might harbour damp or induce mould. Brass wire trellises were used to permit ventilation. The air of the rooms was strictly controlled, the temperature and dryness being regulated. Beckford was very displeased when people mishandled his books, and admitted that at Cintra one day he 'snapped at the Marquis and cast an evil look on the Prior' because they were not treating a precious volume with the respect it deserved. His enthusiasm for his books was limitless. Count Fries's three folio volumes of engravings of Vandykes were, he exclaimed to a visitor, fit to make one 'fall down and worship; such glorious impressions are nowhere to be found!'

We know the name of every single one of the 9,837 books Beckford owned at the time of his death from Bohn's Hamilton Palace catalogue made for the 1882–3 sale at Sotheby's. The majority of them dated from the sixteenth to the eighteenth centuries, being specimens of famous binders of the past. The minority were contemporary. Their subjects covered a very wide range: chiefly the Greek and Latin classics, architecture, travel, engravings of paintings, theology, European literature, contemporary English poetry, witchcraft and the bizarre. Volumes such as *Mélanges Erotiques – Raison pourquoy les Femmes ne portent Barbe au Menton aussi bien qu' à la Penillière* (1601) were few. More fascinating for him was the frankly horrifying in all its manifestations. T. Hall's *Loathsomeness of Long Haire, with an Appendix against Painting, Spots, naked Breasts, etc* (1654) is a mild example. Books on ontology, magic and daemonology – *The Damnable Life of Dr. Faustus* – excited his curiosity. He was highly critical of whatever he found pretentious or merely silly. In J. Brasbridge's *Fruits of Experience* he scribbled, 'They who like Hog-Wash, and there are amateurs for everything, will not turn away disappointed or disgusted with this book, but relish the stale, trashy anecdotes it contains, and gobble them up with avidity.'

Indeed Beckford's marginal comments and remarks pencilled in a crabbed hand often at considerable length on endpapers of books or separate sheets subsequently included in re-binding have become famous among bibliophiles. At the Hamilton Palace sale those books containing his jottings often fetched higher prices on this account alone. And Bohn transcribed many of them in seven folio volumes. It is a great pity that the present whereabouts of 'Transcripts from the autograph Notes written by Mr. Beckford' is unknown.

As he grew older so Beckford's comments became more caustic. Nevertheless his remarks on the books of his contemporaries, though usually bitter and often unjust, are trenchant, and always entertaining. He could criticize from strength other people's books of travel and adventure. Of Colonel Vyse's *Operations at the Pyramids of Gizeh in 1837* he had this to say : 'Boring without end – boring – boring – boring – nothing but boring – and all to very little purpose – or no purpose – the thirstiest desert is not drier than Colonel Vyse's narrative.' Of women writers he was particularly scathing. On the flyleaf of Mary Shelley's *Frankenstein*, a story one might have expected him to enjoy, he wrote, 'This is, perhaps, the foulest toadstool that has yet sprung up from the reeking dunghill of the present times. W.B.' Lady Morgan comes off more lightly with her *Life of Salvator Rosa*. He merely expressed 'contempt and horror' of her 'cuckoo note . . . of commonplace abuse of all constituted authorities and hackneyed incitements to revolution,' and her 'festoons of tinsel and artificial flowers.'

William Hazlitt's *Lectures on English Comic Writers* (1819) actually received commendation. 'A richer vein of bold original criticism and sparkling allusions than is contained in these lectures is not to be found in any volume I am acquainted with.' These words were written before Hazlitt's extremely ungracious remarks about Beckford's collections were published in *Sketches of the Principal Picture Galleries in England* in 1824. Beckford was not the man to overlook an unsolicited injury. Hazlitt's *Journey through France and Italy* of 1826 thereupon received six pages of vitriolic abuse.

Although an avid reader of poetry Beckford was seldom edified by that of his contemporaries. When John Galt, author of *The Annals of the Parish*, unwisely ventured into verse Beckford tersely called it 'about as harmonious as the screeching and grating of the wheels of a Portuguese dray.' Southey's 'All for Love' was described as 'All for Pelf . . . Nothing but the desire of his adding to his stock of pence, and laudable view of presenting to his little friends, sweet listening dears – with comfits of sugar plums, could have induced the Laureate to put forth such a doodlesome publication.' And all that Leigh Hunt's *The Story of Rimini* provoked was 'Mimmini Pimmini.' Unfortunately the cataloguer did not transcribe the notes Beckford made against Keat's *Endymion* or the '7 pages of sarcastic notes' on Lord Byron's collected works. The author of the 'Field of Waterloo' inspired the lines:

The corpse of many a hero slain
Pressed Waterloo's ensanguined plain;
But none by sabre, or by shot,
Fell half so flat as Walter Scott.

And as for William Blake, whose *The Book of Thel* and *The Marriage of Heaven and Hell* were among the bibliophile's treasured volumes, Beckford trounced 'the mad draughtsman's' divine 'Tiger, Tiger burning bright' poem with 'Surely the receiver and disseminator of such trash is as bad as the thief who seems to have stolen them from the walls of Bedlam.' From someone so responsive to the innocent sensibilities of childhood this comment is sadly obtuse. A summary at the end of Shelley's *Queen Mab* edition of 1821, although hostile, is not wholly unfair, coming from a man of over sixty who had witnessed at close quarters the appalling vandalism of the French Revolution.

Verses of such power and tendency, are well worthy to obtain the highest premium from the Satanic School, the first moment that, thanks to the liberality and tolerance of the present æra, these evil genii become a body corporate arrayed in direct opposition to our moral and religious societies. This is indeed the very sort of production which may be supposed to have come forth on the eve of the avenging Deluge, just before the second father of mankind entered the Ark, when the original milk of human kindness had stiffened into a poisonous curd, and the abominable human animal, drunk with crime and with arrogance, with the strength of the Lion and the hoofs of the Ass, kicking off every trammel, pillaged, tortured and violated without restraint, spat in the face of Nature, and denied his God.

Of all the devastating, fulminating diatribes of contempt penned since Dr. Johnson's letter to Lord Chesterfield, surely Beckford's concluding note in Gibbon's *Decline and Fall* is without an equal.

The time is not far distant, Mr. Gibbon, when your almost ludicrous self-complacency, your numerous, and sometimes apparently wilful mistakes, your frequent distortion of historical Truth to provoke a jibe, or excite a sneer at everything most sacred and venerable, your ignorance of the oriental languages, your limited and far from acutely critical knowledge of the Latin and the Greek, and in the midst of all the prurient and obscene gossip of your notes – your affected moral purity perking up every now and then from the corrupt mass like artificial roses shaken off in the dark by some Prostitute on a heap of manure, your heartless scepticism, your unclassical fondness for meretricious ornament, your tumid diction, your monotonous jingle of periods, will be still more exposed and scouted than they have been. Once fairly kicked off from your lofty, bedizened stilts, you will be reduced to your just level and true standard. W.B.

In one way and another W.B. had his full measure of revenge against the man who once rashly snubbed a fellow guest at the Duchess of Devonshire's party for mentioning in his presence the name of so outrageous person as Mr. Beckford.

108

160 — — A very good looking waiter — (who by the
way says Marianne was particularly remarkable
for the elegant expression of his Countenance & the
regularity of his truly grecian features) told me
that the heat of last summer at Turin had been
so oppressive that he had scarcely been able to
taste food during its continuance — —

171 At Settimo, Marianne spied out a beautiful
girl with the fine grecian line of features — long oval
Cheek, dark pale skin (fine & smooth as mellow'd
ivory) curled red lips with long soft black eyes and
straight eyebrows. —

172 Mr. B. at the Opera at Turin feeling something
tickle his forehead, put up his hand & caught hold
of a monstrous black Spider at least four inches
in circumference. — —

177 Lovely cherubim faces & silken locks; but
also not kept free from dirt and — worse
than Dirt — —

190 Our animated authoress is deservedly fortunate
in meeting with handsome waiters & lovely objects
of both sexes — at Milan she was quite enraptured
with two or three charming Women; one in particular
a true madonna of Correggio who if seen in a
London circle wd have created an immense sensation —

205 More pretty faces & more bad smells — Marianne
206 never forgets to mention either — —

230 Marianne asked her Host of la Croix blanche at
Sion what was the chief manufacture of the place
to which he replied with a ridiculous shrug of the
Shoulders Des Enfans —

267 The P.V. superior to most waterfalls — —
— the P.V. how modern, how pretty — — —
Madde. de Genlis or any of the french Scribblers

To Beckford, whose giants among poets were Shakespeare, Milton, Dante and Quevedo, the midgets who followed them were totally unworthy of any consideration whatever. Lesser men of letters were in his opinion beyond the pale of consideration. Farington opined that he was jealous of everyone who excelled, for his disposition was unamiable. There is something in the charge. Beckford never went to school, and never learnt the give and take of competition. Vain rather than conceited he was reluctant to concede to others talents which he enjoyed and of which a cruel misfortune had until his old age withheld from him the world's approbation. The only contemporary writers among his compatriots whom he grudgingly admired were Byron and Disraeli, both younger men than himself. His attitude to Byron was ambivalent. He refused to meet him when the poet pressed his friend Rogers to bring about an introduction, and when in 1832 Murray printed Byron's suppressed stanza 'Dives' about Beckford's homosexuality, he was grievously offended. On learning of the poet's death in 1824 he exclaimed, 'So Byron is gone. He cared about the world, affected not to care, defied it and was unsuccessful. I have defied it and succeeded. I have resources if I should live centuries . . .' The remark is poignant in that the maker of it was deceiving himself by a bravado he could not truthfully sustain. In Disraeli he saw someone very much younger than himself whom he would not live long enough to find a serious rival. Besides he detected in the early novels of the cocksure young Disraeli the work of a disciple, and was flattered. When they met at the opera in 1834 both men were a trifle disappointed. Beckford was put off by Dizzy's flamboyance and reports of his smoking; which put an absolute veto on his ever being received at Lansdown Crescent. Dizzy's note in his diary was patronising. He found the Caliph 'very bitter and malin, but full of warm feelings for the worthy'.

Once Beckford was established in Bath he embarked upon the prolonged process of looking through papers and writings to which old men are prone. In 1824 he issued a new edition of *Biographical Memoirs of Extraordinary Painters* which had first been published forty-four years previously. In the early 1830s he was busily amending *Dreams, Waking Thoughts and Incidents*, which had been suppressed in 1783. He submitted a revised version to his bookseller Clarke. Clarke offered it to the publisher Bentley, who asked that it should be expanded. After some demurring and haggling on Beckford's part he accordingly fished out and largely recast the travel diaries kept in Portugal and Spain in 1787–8. The result was that in 1834 Bentley published both works in two volumes as *Italy; with Sketches of Spain and Portugal by the author of Vathek*. They were rapturously received by the critics. Lockhart in the *Quarterly Review* (vol. 51. 1834) declared that 'Mr Beckford's book is entirely unlike any book of travels *in prose* that exists in any European language,' continuing:

His rapture amidst the sublime scenery of mountains and forests . . . is that of a spirit cast originally in one of nature's finest moulds; and he fixes it in language which can scarcely be praised beyond its deserts – simple, massive, nervous, apparently little laboured, yet revealing, in its effect, the perfection of art.

Greatly encouraged by the reception of the two volumes the author of *Vathek* published in the following year his *Recollections of an Excursion to the Monasteries of Alcobaça and Batalha*, which was greeted by the public with no less enthusiasm. *The Gentleman's Magazine* (September 1835) referred to the author's

deep sensibility to all that is beautiful in nature and art, rich romantic imagination, fine and finished taste, humour most elegant and playful, all mixed up with a wild and fastidious melancholy.

This was the last of his books published in the author's lifetime. Beckford's literary artistry was as sure as ever when he came to recapture those cherished memories of a distant past. But the creative spark was extinct. Small wonder, for he was in his seventy-sixth year. The manuscript he left behind, to be published by Guy Chapman in 1930 under the title *Liber Veritatis*, is a sad falling off in Beckford's literary output. All one can say is that he had the sense not to risk publication in his lifetime. The subject of the work is, as the editor explained, 'the child of an obsession.' The *Liber Veritatis* consists of a chain of discreditable anecdotes intended to debunk the lineage of the new aristocracy. It does not require a psychoanalyst to point out that these captious jottings reflect Beckford's hankering after his lost peerage, and nagging grievance over his ill treatment by society, from which he could never escape even towards the end of a long life.

8 · WINTER OF DISCONTENT

HOSE few persons who paid visits to Beckford in Lansdown Crescent or at the tower and left written records gave a very different impression of their host from what we deduce from the prickly, malign and embittered pages of the *Liber Veritatis*. They depict him as exceedingly courteous, charitable, sweet-tempered and conciliatory, with just a touch of mischief in his disposition to make him all the more endearing. How far were they right? First, we must bear in mind that they were rather unsophisticated, socially undistinguished and, if not all less intelligent then certainly less sharp than he was: Cyrus Redding, his future biographer, a provincial journalist and prolific author of light literature; Mr. Lansdown, a courtly, elderly gentleman disposed to see the best in everybody; Jerom Murch, an employee of the Bath City Council, who after serving seven times as Mayor, published *Biographical Sketches of Bath Celebrities* in 1893; Edmund F. English, the auctioneer and furniture dealer of Milsom Street; and H. E. Goodridge, Beckford's architect. These men were in a sense necessarily subservient. They were flattered to be received by the rich recluse who was a distinguished author with a spicy history of so many decades ago that they had little inkling what it amounted to. That Beckford was welcoming and polite to his social and intellectual inferiors from whom he had nothing to fear goes without saying. But charitable and sweet-tempered he certainly was not. An afternoon's tour conducted by the great man himself round his house, during which he expatiated delightfully and knowledgeably on the incomparable works of art it contained, revealed few traces of the bitterness of his inmost soul, the scars from the injuries he had suffered, the rages to which he occasionally gave open vent and the vilification of his enemies to which he gave expression on paper. Of those persons we have mentioned probably Goodridge alone had any experience of Beckford's satanic side. And he affirmed that during the Bath years his client's rages gradually abated. Even so in April 1843, a year before his death, Beckford wrote furiously to Goodridge of his intention of quitting Bath for ever, 'having been most grievously disturbed early this morning by the noise of dogs.'

Of course he had no intention of doing any such thing. Once only during the Bath years he seriously intended going abroad again. In 1826 he spent six months packing and preparing his vast retinue for a trip to Rome. He even got as far as London, where he changed his mind, and returned. It was all too troublesome. He could not face it. He seldom went anywhere but to London now. He rented a succession of houses in the capital, no. 127 Park Street, W.1. ('Cesspool House') being the last. Young

W. P. Frith caught a glimpse of him in Phillips's, the Bond Street auctioneer's rooms, around 1837. He was 'a short man, dressed in a green coat with brass buttons, leather breeches and top-boots, and his hair was powdered,' which was remarkable enough to make him look very old-fashioned. Indeed another observer thought his dress resembled that of a well-to-do farmer. He was staring at a picture and Frith heard him ejaculating, 'That damned thing a Raphael! Great heavens, think of that now! Can there be such damned fools as to believe that a Raphael! What a damned fool I was to come here!' It is doubtful whether the respectable Messrs. Redding, Murch and English overheard such exclamations as these in Lansdown Crescent. The habit of talking to himself as though he were alone, even when others were present, was a habit he developed. It was particularly noticeable when he was walking and riding, or otherwise abstracted.

Hardly a soul came to stay in the last years, apart from the Duke and Duchess of Hamilton. Beckford was fond enough of his daughter with whom he had little in common, for she was not particularly clever. She was conventional and sweet, and returned more affection than she received. With his son-in-law he shared many interests. The 10th Duke of Hamilton was, like him, intensely proud of his descent, and madly addicted to heraldry and genealogy. He too was a connoisseur of the arts and a distinguished collector of illuminated manuscripts. Underneath an almost ludicrous pomposity (Beckford referred to him, not however to his face, as the Arcadian Shepherd, a nicely grotesque allusion), the Duke had romantic tendencies which got him into political trouble. He was a dedicated Buonapartist, even going to the limits of having an affair with Napoleon's sister Pauline Borghese at the moment when England was fighting the Corsican tyrant for very existence. The scandal appealed to Beckford's love of mischief. He did not live quite long enough to relish the scandal of his granddaughter Lady Lincoln's elopement and divorce from her husband. On the other hand his grandson William Alexander, later 11th Duke of Hamilton's marriage to a daughter of the reigning Grand Duke of Baden brought him more satisfaction than it did to the bride or bridegroom.

A blackamoor stool, formerly in Beckford's possession, now at Brodick Castle.

Samuel Rogers ('The Yellow One') repeated his visits to Beckford at Fonthill by another to Lansdown Crescent, at his own invitation. It does not seem to have been so successful as the previous ones. Beckford shocked his guest not a little by reading aloud extracts from the *Episodes of Vathek* (first published in 1912) with their homosexual connotations. He had been incensed with Rogers's friend Tom Moore, whose help he had begged The Yellow One in 1818 to enlist in the publication of his travel diaries. Moore had declined out of prudish reasons; and Beckford suspected that Rogers failed to press his friend sufficiently. At any rate in the copy of Rogers's *Human Life* Beckford scribbled tartly, 'I rather think we also have received Mr. Rogers's little all.' Only a handful of metropolitan writers

113

called upon him from time to time, including Harrison Ainsworth and Mrs. (C. G. F.) Gore, authoress of *Cecil, or the Adventures of a Coxcomb*, a novel about Mayfair social life, for which she claimed to be indebted to Beckford.

And what of Gregorio Franchi during these years, the loyal Franchi, whom at the age of seventeen 'I loaded . . . with childish caresses,' in between bouts of harpsichord playing and madrigal singing in the Quinta dos Bichos as long ago as 1787; Franchi who abandoned a wife and daughter for his sake, who never thereafter left him except to run errands in London and Paris, buying for him books, pictures and treasures of all sorts; in whom Beckford confided his inmost thoughts and desires; Franchi who acted as indispensable secretary, supervised the enormous households at Fonthill and in Bath; who was always laughing and constantly good-tempered; who reconciled warring factions among the indoor and outdoor servants and kept everybody happy; who won the love of the Hamiltons and interceded with the proud Duke, invariably successfully, on Beckford's behalf after family rows? On 4th November 1817 we have Beckford writing him a letter of genuine affection and concern about his poor health.

Be assured that I would rather be beside you, bereft of everything, halt and maimed, in preference to the most splendid position in the universe amidst the gayest company. Not a moment of my life passes without your being present before my eyes.

Alas, for the fickleness of human relations! Poor Franchi became a martyr to gout and arthritis, and is last heard of languishing in poverty in a London lodging house, while his master and friend remained shut up amidst the comforts of Lansdown Crescent. In the greatest distress and agonising pain he died in 1828. Beckford never went to cheer him, never so much as wrote him a line. And the reason? The sensitive Caliph could not bear unpleasantnesses of any sort. It is difficult not to think the less of him for such callous indifference towards the best friend he ever had.

No wonder Beckford found old age a melancholy business. Besides it was humiliating. 'I am really ashamed of being so old,' he exclaimed to one visitor. Like all superannuated men he worried deeply over the future of his country, and after the passing of the Reform Bill foresaw nothing but disaster ahead. In 1842 he found a morbid solace in designing and having erected in the shadow of his tower a pink granite tomb for his remains. He much disliked the idea of being buried under the earth. The sarcophagus was placed beside the grave of Tiny, his adored spaniel, who had succeeded the terrier Tout in his unbounded affections. That year he derived a good deal of pleasure in buying a bronze bust of Caligula with silver eyes, which had been one of Horace Walpole's greatest treasures. To acquire things which had belonged to and been cherished by people he cordially disliked satisfied his odd motives of revenge. Actually Walpole

114

Beckford's tomb in Lansdown Cemetery in the shadow of the Tower. Designed by himself, it is of pink polished granite with bronze armorial plaques and inscriptions.

Bronze armorial bearings and inscription on one end of Beckford's tomb.

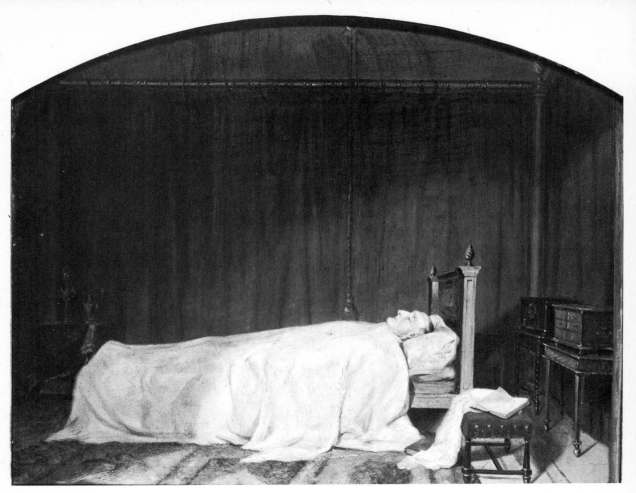

Beckford on his deathbed, in an austere room in Lansdown Crescent. At the head and foot of the bed are some of his treasured possessions. By Willes Maddox, now at Brodick Castle.

endeavoured to bequeath his possessions so that they might be beyond Beckford's reach. The irony of the sequel was that Beckford outlived Walpole's heirs.

In April 1844 he made the greatest mistake of his life. He went for a walk in the east wind, and got drenched to the skin. Fever set in. He was frightened, and clamoured for his daughter Susan. He was just able to hold a pen. 'O abrégez la distance . . . O abrégez la fatale distance,' he wrote. They had always corresponded in French. Susan dutifully rushed to his bedside. 'Je ne suis pas las de vivre mais le vivre est las de moi,' were almost his last words. The rector of the parish called, but Beckford would not see him. On 2nd May he died, and Willes Maddox was summoned to make an oil sketch of the death chamber. So the last view we have is of Beckford lying on a narrow wooden bed, a sheet up to his sharply projecting chin, in an austere, pictureless room, hung with a lugubrious crimson curtain, an open book on the stool beside him, two little caskets (in one of which, now at Brodick Castle, he kept Alexander Cozens's letters) on tables behind his head, and what look like precious ewers or beakers at his feet.

116

'I can hardly conceive a pleasanter spot to lie quiet in than the summit of Lansdown,' Beckford had written. Yet because the spot was unhallowed ground and because the propinquity of poor Tiny's grave was deemed unfitting, they buried him ten days after his death in Lyncombe Vale Cemetery, having first moved there the heavy granite monument. The coffin of Spanish mahogany, embellished with gilded armorials specially designed by the deceased, was borne along Lansdown Crescent, down Lansdown Road and Milsom Street, across Pulteney Bridge and along Pulteney Street. The immensely long cortège, attended by the Duke and Duchess of Hamilton, the Marquess of Douglas and his wife the Princess of Baden, the Countess of Lincoln and Beckford's own empty carriage, and preceded by a tall mourner carrying a black plume of ostrich feathers attached to a board the size and shape of a coffin lid, passed between rows of Bathonians gathered to witness the impressive obsequies in honour of the legendary recluse, who for many years had dwelt, little seen and seldom approached, in their city.

In November 1845 an eight-day sale took place of nos. 19 and 20 Lansdown Crescent, the tower and those contents which did not find their way to Hamilton Palace. In 1848 Duchess Susan piously bought back Lansdown Tower and part of the garden which she presented to Walcot parish for use as a cemetery. At her wish the pink sarcophagus was re-erected on the very spot chosen by her father, which was now consecrated ground, and the coffin duly put inside it. There it has remained to this day.

Joseph Farington having specified in his diary a number of Beckford's less amiable qualities, concluded thus: 'You see the character is irregular by looking in his countenance, there is a twist in his look.' He does not explain what he meant by the word 'twist'. Beckford's countenance was not what the French call *chétif*, sly or foxy. It was on the contrary direct, bold and at times insolent. But it was inscrutable for it concealed ambiguities. As this brief account of his life has unfolded, his impulses have emerged as unpredictable, and often paradoxical. If his character was irregular it was also astonishingly contradictory. Loathing all forms of physical cruelty, he was fascinated by the sadistic and macabre, as is evident from his choice of books and reading. He was violent and gentle. He treated his servants to cuffs at one moment and guineas the next. Exacting master that he was, he trusted them implicitly in leaving loose jewels in bowls and vases for any thief to purloin. The result was that no thief ever did. In fact his servants remained with him for years. He resolutely refused to support the anti-slavery movement, yet loudly deprecated the worsening status under Pitt's government of the agricultural labourers. During a bad winter at Fonthill he bought and distributed among his poorer tenantry hundreds of pairs of blankets and waggon loads of coal. On leaving Fonthill he gave twenty acres to the humbler inhabitants of Hindon to enable them to grow vegetables. He paid

The black ebony casket (shown on the right of Maddox's deathbed picture) in which Beckford in boyhood kept the letters he received from Alexander Cozens.

the workmen engaged on his various buildings inordinately high wages which they spent on drink, and then sacked them for their intemperance. He railed against the social injustice which allowed the Bishop of Clogher, after his arrest on a charge of unnatural vice, to flee abroad, while the waiter Eglerton ('a poor honest sodomite') was publically executed in spite of the pleas of his devoted wife and children.

Beckford's standard of honesty was very strict. He was punctilious in settling accounts. Whatever he bought he paid for before taking it away. He drove a hard bargain and exacted the last farthing from anyone who owed him money. He was shamelessly hypocritical in acquiring the gift of some diamonds from an old woman by pretending to love her cats. As we have seen, he was spendthrift and mean, generous and miserly. He had intellectual integrity and yet was a slave to social conventions. He was an aristocrat in that his mode of life and apparent indifference to the opinion of the multitude were those of the *grand seigneur*; and yet he was no gentleman when we consider his behaviour towards individuals, his daughter Margaret and the dying Franchi.

His unresolved attitude to religion is a key to the discontent which poisoned his whole life. He had a strong inclination to Christianity but no religious faith. He was by nature sceptical and contemptuous of superstition. He could not bring himself to believe in salvation and yet, like Byron, he believed in damnation and hell. In this as in so many other respects the two were extraordinarily alike, and it was perhaps no coincidence that the mothers of both these fatherless geniuses were puritanical Scots. It was in vain that Beckford derided the Begum's 'methodistical' upbringing, her admonitions to her son not to run the risks of everlasting fire and brimstone, and her fulminous quotations from the Old Testament. He could not escape from her deeply engrained influences. His terrible poem 'Dies Irae' is sufficient testimony of that dread of eternal retribution which haunted him.

> Hark! heard ye not that deep appalling sound?
> Tremble! – for lo, the vex'd, the affrighted ground
> Heaves strong in dread convulsion – streams of fire
> Burst from the vengeful sky – a voice of ire
> Proclaims, 'Ye guilty, wait your final doom:
> No more the silent refuge of the tomb
> Shall screen your crimes, your frailties. Conscience reigns –
> Earth needs no other sceptre – what remains
> Beyond her fated limits, dare not tell; –
> Eternal justice! Judgement! Heaven! – Hell!

Beckford implicitly believed that men needed a disciplinary system within which to exercise their religious practices. He saw the most efficacious system to be the Roman Catholic Church, with its long unbroken history in the west, and its power to instil supernatural faith and terror. He could not find this necessary straitjacket in the Church

of England. He despised and even loathed Protestantism, and never refrained from explaining why. A reference to Salisbury Cathedral in a letter to Franchi of 1st June 1808 is unequivocal:

I've always found the said Cathedral poor, bare and insipid, without mystery, without ecclesiastical pomp; only the tower is any good. Bagasse [Wyatt's] work there is infamous. Oh the disgust and stink of Protestantism (it doesn't deserve the sonorous name of Heresy). All these windows, all this light, all this glass with its small diamond-shaped panes make this shameless church look like a whore clad only in muslin – what an infamous spot. How I abhor it . . .

Only a year before he had pronounced similar strictures upon Westminster Abbey:

If the building was purged by celestial Catholic fire of all the foulness of infamous Protestantism it would be capable of producing the most majestic effect imaginable.

And in 1811 he wrote,

Ah, if only they had the good sense to restore the true Faith in all its venerable splendour – what a paradise this earth would become.

The artist in Beckford was of course drawn to Catholicism by the ritual, 'the ceremonial observances . . . into the real meaning of which so few

The railings which surrounded Beckford's tomb while it was temporarily in Lyncombe Vale Cemetery. When Goodridge built the gateway to Lansdown Cemetery in 1848 he incorporated them in the flanking walls.

119

have the candour to enquire,' the lavish ornaments, vestments, incense and all the pomp and trappings of triumphalism. And why on earth not? These allurements were deliberately introduced by the Catholic Church in order to win the masses to the true Faith, as pollen is meant to draw bees, and thereby elicit tribute to the glory of God. More is perhaps needed to sustain man's allegiance to Catholicism, but the blind acceptance of dogma which the Church demanded aroused no response in Beckford. His approach to religion was both too emotional and too subjective. For example, his devotion to St. Antony of Padua, undoubtedly sincere, was probably motivated by self-identification with this holy aristocrat who had turned aside from a society he found uncongenial to preach truth to a whole European generation. Even so Beckford treated the saint rather like one of his pet dogs, with a sort of offhand manner which was as much affectionate as devotional, amused as reverential.

André Parreaux is right in supposing that for Beckford religion which did not inspire art was no true religion. Nevertheless I believe that Beckford required an additional element to art through which to attain spiritual fulfilment. If the masterpieces of architecture, painting and music were not enough, there was nature undefiled by man. Beckford's dependence upon the untrammelled green earth and illimitable blue sky sets him in a separate genre from writers like, say, Sydney Smith and Ronald Firbank, whose horizons were artificial, man-made barriers. Indeed 'prayer,' he wrote, 'does not always ascend with the greatest fervency from beneath gilded vaults or gorgeous cupolas; it is in the free untainted desert, under Nature's own sky, that man seems to commune more deeply with his God.' Beckford's religion, in so far as he had one at all, was a sort of vague pantheism. It was in universal nature that he sought union with the divine. And it is not without significance that in his library he had the works of the greatest Christian thinker along pantheistic lines, St. Dionysius the Areopagite, and of the most thorough-going exponent of pantheism in modern times, Spinoza. Beckford liked too to indulge in a little pagan play-acting. When on approaching Rome for the first time he caught sight of St. Peter's dome, the mecca of that Catholic Church which he so deeply venerated, he stopped by a stream, and 'poured water upon my hands, and then lifting them up to the sylvan genii of the place, implored their protection.'

If we need any further indication of Beckford's equivocal attitude to religion and his pathetic doubts and hopes we have merely to turn to the 'Prayer' he composed. It is not very good poetry and is too long to quote fully. But the last lines express a fervent evocation to the 'All pervading Spirit – Sacred Beam, parent of life and light', and end with the words he had inscribed upon his tomb:

Eternal Power!
Grant me through obvious clouds one transient gleam
of thy bright essence in my dying hour.

120

Like all people who want to be religious and cannot, Beckford was a tormented man. Unlike the happy atheist without a care for the future and with a blissful insouciance in the face of total annihilation, he was perplexed, to put it mildly, by the purpose of life and the consequence of death. Cyrus Redding realized that in his old age he was profoundly dissatisfied with his past life. He had not attained his early ambitions as a writer. What writer ever does attain them? His art collections only gave him moments of transient pleasure in the way a good meal gives pleasure to a gourmet. He found connoisseurship much less satisfactory than creation. He used constantly to murmur, Redding recorded, 'Cui bono? Cui bono?' He vaguely hoped that the acquisition of knowledge was a good thing in itself. As a non-conformist to the shibboleths of his class he had to bear the perpetual cross of its suspicion and dislike. He pretended not to care but in truth the hostility of his fellow men was a nagging pain. In one sense he made the Powderham scandal an excuse for his temperamental shortcomings. It was founded on such intolerable injustice and falsehood, he maintained, that he was driven to defensive measures against society at large. So he fell back upon, almost revelled in that terrible, injurious discontent, which in recollecting those summer days of Portugal in 1787 he referred to as 'the germ of destructiveness, which might then have been trodden down [but] has arisen into a tree fraught with poisons, darkening the wholesome light, and receiving nourishment, through all its innumerable fibres, from the lowest depths of hell.' That hell threatened by the Begum might have been averted if only he had seized the opportunities Marialva offered him, position, a title, and all the delirious privileges of pantomime life in that delicious 'fag end of Europe', Portugal. Instead of which he had chosen to return to the land of his birth, Gothic England of fog and fury, there to assume as an act of defiance the role of despotic caliph and, again like Byron, make himself out to be thought worse than he was. Redding was a perspicacious man, albeit an inaccurate biographer when it came to facts. Of all the strange stories of Fonthill which circulated, 'differing as they did,' he said, 'there was one point upon which all agreed; and that was that Mr. Beckford was the type of his own Vathek – a half human, half demon sort of being.' It came about that he exalted the role to a height of sublimity; and for anyone 'to abuse Vathek he deemed [it] a personal insult.'

William Beckford was the quintessential romantic, the eternal child, for ever playing a role. In looking back upon childhood as the only happy dream he anticipated the Wordsworth of *The Prelude*. But unlike Wordsworth's his dreams were not limited to what had happened in the distant past, but extended to what should still be happening in the present. The adult who tries to combat the harsh realities of life with the illusions of childhood only has himself to blame when these illusions turn to smoke. Beckford's particular brand of love was that of a protective elder brother for a younger. What Prince Alasi was towards Firouz in the

Episodes of Vathek, he, Beckford, had been to Kitty Courtenay and Dom Pedro. In these callow boys he saw a projection of himself. In searching for his own lost innocence in them he was deceived. Innocence of the loved ones projected by the lover turned to guile. In consequence Beckford suffered from guilt over transformations which were none of his wishing, but for which he believed himself to be somehow responsible. Guile in the loved ones and guilt in the lover were the invariable outcome of pledges of eternal union with unworthy objects. Disillusion and bitterness were all that remained long after the episodes were over and forgotten. No appeals to his revered St. Antony, the recoverer of lost trifles, including hearts, could find him a way out of this predicament.

His daughter the Duchess of Hamilton remarked after her father's death, 'He used to say, "What are forms? The heart is everything." ' Here we have the disingenuous child, the self-dramatizer. In 1787 he wrote, 'It is amazing how I enjoy getting into scrapes. To me a scrape is like a dram. It raises my spirits and brightens my imagination.' And here we have the provocative child, the self-destroyer. It is all very well to defy society provided you are impervious to society's revenges. Beckford was innately custom-bound and thin-skinned. It took him over half a century to grow a carapace of indifference to the world's opinion; even then he had his Achilles' heel. It was an extreme sensitivity to the snubs of individuals.

As writer, builder and collector Beckford was, as far as style goes, ahead of his time. He could not by any stretch of exaggeration be termed a philosopher. Yet throughout his long life he was the consistent champion of the right of every man to his own opinions and conduct, so long as no harm was thereby caused to others. At times he lacked the courage of his convictions and kept his mouth shut when he should have spoken out. But he never wavered in his convictions. The man whom Byron uncharitably dubbed the 'apostle of pederasty' was the apostle of free thinking and free living. It is perhaps this aspect of him which appeals as much as any other to the present generation.

It may sound absurd to compare William Beckford to his exact contemporary, William Blake. The two men, one extremely rich, the other a near pauper, had diametrically opposed backgrounds and temperaments. But they shared one thing in common – and that was a new intellectual integrity. Each rejected the old, stilted, artificial means of disguising intellectual truths. Blake's methods of building Jerusalem in England's green and pleasant land were biblical and spiritual. Beckford's were pagan and physical. Yet each propounded them in ways that were absolutely heartfelt and honest.

122

BIBLIOGRAPHY

Alexander, Boyd (ed.), *The Journal of William Beckford in Portugal and Spain 1787–1788* (with Introduction), 1954.

Alexander, Boyd, *Life at Fonthill . . . 1807–1822*, 1957.

Alexander, Boyd, 'Beckford's Taste', *History Today*, October, 1960.

Alexander, Boyd (ed.), *Beckford's Journal of 1794*, 1961.

Alexander, Boyd, 'William Beckford as Patron', *Apollo*, July, 1962.

Alexander, Boyd, *England's Wealthiest Son*, 1962.

Alexander, Boyd, 'Fonthill, Wiltshire, II' and 'III. The Abbey and Its Creator', *Country Life*, 1 and 8 Dec., 1966.

Bell, C. R., *Memoirs of J. R. Cozens in The Catalogue of his Drawings*, Burlington Club, 1922–3.

Bell, C. R. and T. Girtin, *Drawings and Sketches of J. R. Cozens*, Walpole Soc. xxiii, 1935.

Britton, John, *Graphical and Literary Illustrations of Fonthill*, 1823.

Britton, John, *Autobiography*, 1850.

Brockman, H. A. N., *The Caliph of Fonthill*, 1956.

Chapman, Guy (ed.), *'The Vision' and 'Liber Veritatis' by William Beckford of Fonthill* (with Introduction and Notes), 1930.

Chapman, Guy, *Beckford*, 1937.

Clark, Kenneth, *The Gothic Revival*, 1928.

Crallan, Hugh, 'Beckford's Houses in Bath', *Architectural Rev.*, March, 1968.

Dale, Anthony, *James Wyatt*, 1956.

Eastlake, C. L., *A History of the Gothic Revival*, 1874.

English, Edmund F., *Views of Lansdown Tower by Willes Maddox*, 1844.

Farington, Joseph, *Diary of 1792–1821* (abridged in 8 published vols. 1923–8 and 28 vols. of typescript in Print Room, British Museum).

Fothergill, Brian, 'William Beckford, Prince of Amateurs', Roy. Soc. of Literature, *Essays from Divers Hands*, 1973.

Frith, W. P., *My Autobiography* (vol. 2), 1888.

Gemmett, R. J. (ed.), *Sale Catalogues of Eminent Persons, vol. 3, Beckford*, 1972.

Gregory, W., *The Beckford Family*, 1898.

Greville, Hon. C., Letter of 25 Dec., 1784 to Sir Wm. Hamilton (see Morrison Letters).

Harris, J., 'Fonthill, Wiltshire 1. Alderman Beckford's Houses', *Country Life*, 24 Nov., 1966.

Hazlitt, William, *Sketches of the Principal Picture Galleries of England*, 1824.

Herrmann, Frank, *The English as Collectors*, 1972.

Higginson, A. H., *Peter Beckford, Esquire*, 1937.

Hobson, A.R.A., *William Beckford's Binders*, Stuttgart, 1961.

Hussey, Christopher, *The Picturesque*, 1927.

Jay, Rev. William, *Autobiography and Reminiscences*, 1854.

Jones, Thomas, *Memoirs, 1742–1803*, Walpole Soc., xxxii, 1951.

Lansdown, Mr., *Recollections of the Late William Beckford*, 1893.

Lees-Milne, James, 'Blake and Beckford' (T.V. broadcast), 1967.

Leveson-Gower, Lord Granville, *Private Correspondence* (vol. 2), 28 Oct., 1817.

Loudon, J. C., Articles on Beckford and Fonthill Abbey, *Gardener's Magazine*, Sept., 1835 and Sept., 1836.

Macaulay, Rose, *They Went to Portugal*, 1946.

Mahmoud, F. M., *William Beckford of Fonthill* (Bicentenary Essays) 1960.

Maslen, B. J., 'Beckford', *Musical Opinion* (Pamphlet xi), May, 1933.

Meehan, J. F., *Famous Houses of Bath*, 1901.

Melville, Lewis, *Life and Letters of William Beckford*, 1910.

Melville, Lewis (ed.), *The Episodes of Vathek*, 1912.

Mitford, Rev. John, 'Recollections of Beckford' (Notebooks B.M.Ad. MSS 32566–7).

Morrison Letters, *Hamilton and Nelson Papers*, 2nd ser., vol. 1, no. 133, 1882–93.

Murch, Jerome, *Biographical Sketches of Bath Celebrities*, 1893.

Murphy, J. C., *Plans, Elevations, Sections & Views of the Church of Batalha*, 1795.
Namier, Sir Lewis and John Brooke, *The House of Commons 1754–1790*, vol. 2, 1964.
Nares, Owen, 'Painshill, Surrey, I and II', *Country Life*, 2 and 9 Jan., 1958.
Neale, Erskine, *The Closing Scene*, 1849.
Neale, J. P., *Views of Seats*, article on Fonthill Abbey, 2nd ser. vol. 1., 1824.
Oliver, J. W., *The Life of William Beckford*, 1932.
Oman, Carola, *Nelson*, 1947.
Oppé, A. P., *Alexander and John Robert Cozens*, 1952.
Parreaux, André, *William Beckford, auteur de Vathek*, 1960.
Phillips, Mr., *Catalogue of the Library and Furniture Sale at Fonthill*, 1823.
Pococke, Dr. Richard, *Travels Through England (1754)*, 2 vols., 1888.
Powys, Mrs. Lybbe, *Diaries, 1756–1808*, 1899.
Price, Uvedale, *An Essay on the Picturesque*, 1794.
Quennell, Peter, *Romantic England, 1717–1851*, 1970.
Redding, Cyrus, *Memorials of William Beckford*, 2 vols., 1859.
Roseberry, Eva, 'Books from Beckford's Library', *Book Collector*, xiv, 1965.
Rushout, Hon. Anne, Diaries (unpublished), 1799 and 1822.
Rutter, John, *Delineations of Fonthill & Its Abbey*, 1823.
Sitwell, Sacheverell, *Essay on Beckford and Beckfordism*, 1924.
Sotheby, Wilkinson and Hodge, *Catalogue* (in 4 parts) *of the Beckford Library in the Hamilton Palace Sales*, 1882–4.
Steegman, John, *The Rule of Taste from George I to George IV*, 1936.
Storer, J., *A Description of Fonthill*, 1812.
Summers, Peter, 'William Beckford: Some notes on his life in Bath', *Catalogue of Exhibition in Holburne of Menstrie Museum*, Bath, 1966.
Townshend-Mayer, Mrs. G., 'The Sultan of Lansdown Tower', *Temple Bar*, June, 1910.
Waagen, Dr. G. F., *Works of Art and Artists in England* (vol. 3), 1838.
Wainwright, Clive, 'Some Objects from W. Beckford's Collections now in the Victoria and Albert Museum', *Burlington Magazine*, May, 1971.
Watkin, David, *Thomas Hope*, 1968.
Wilton-Ely, John, 'A Model for Fonthill Abbey', *The Country Seat*, 1970.
Walpole, Horace, *Letters 1732–1797*, 1903–5.
'Lord Nelson's Reception at Fonthill', *Gentleman's Magazine*, vol. 71, 1801.
'A review of *The Vision* and *Liber Veritatis*', *Times Lit. Supplement*, 14 Aug., 1930.

BECKFORD'S PUBLISHED WRITINGS (FIRST ISSUES)

Biographical Memoirs of Extraordinary Painters, begun in 1777 when Beckford was still 16, published anonymously, 1780.
The Vision, written 1777–8, published with *Liber Veritatis* with Introduction and Notes by Guy Chapman, 1930.
An Excursion to the Grande Chartreuse in the Year 1778, printed 1783, published in *Italy with Sketches of Spain and Portugal*, 1834.
Dreams, Waking Thoughts and Incidents, written 1780–3, printed anonymously, 1783. Suppressed. Re-issued in amended form as Vol. 1 of *Italy; with Sketches of Spain and Portugal*, 1834.
Vathek, written 1782. Henley's translation published 1786.
Vathek (in French), published Lausanne, 1787.
The Journal of William Beckford in Portugal and Spain, written 1787–8, published with Introduction and Notes by Boyd Alexander, 1954.
Journal of 1794, edited by Boyd Alexander and published 1961.
Modern Novel Writing, or The Elegant Enthusiast, pseudonym Lady Harriet Marlow, published 1796.
Azemia, pseudonym J. A. M. Jenks, published 1797.
Italy; with Sketches of Spain and Portugal, 2 vols, published 1834.
Recollections of an Excursion to the Monasteries of Alcobaça and Batalha in 1794, published 1835.
The Episodes of Vathek, edited by Lewis Melville and published 1912.
Liber Veritatis, written in the 1830s and published with *The Vision* (see above).

INDEX

Abercorn, 6th Earl of, 11
Aboyne, 4th Earl of (father-in-law), 28
Adam, Robert, 41
Ainsworth, W. Harrison, 114
Alcobaça, monastery of, 38, 40, 95
Alexander, Boyd, 8, 31, 38, 49, 102
Alfieri, Count Vittorio, 7, 35
Allen, Ralph, 77
Amelia, Princess, 56
American Garden, or Plantation, Fonthill, 36, 57, 59
Anastasius (1819), 26
Angell, Joseph, 88, 91
Angus, W. *(Seats)*, 13
Anspach, Margravine of, *see* Craven
Anspach, Margravine of, *see* Germaine
Antiquities of Athens (1762), plate from, 82
Arabian Nights, The, 16, 24, 25
Aranda, Countess of, 35
Aranjuez Palace, Spain, 56
Ashridge Park, Herts., 54, 61, 64
Atkinson, William, 81
Augsburg cabinet, 66
Auguste, R. J., 37
Aviz, Prior of, 38, 106

Bacon, John, 15, 35
Bacon, Roger, 62
Baden, Grand Duke of, 113
Baden, Princess Mary of, 117
Baillie, Marianne *(Tour upon the Continent)*, 109
Banks, Thomas, 15, 35
Barrett, George, jnr., 96
Barry, Sir Charles, 52
Barthélémon, F. H., 26
Batalha, monastery of, 38, 40, 47, 48, 49, 60, 64
Bath, 41, 77 *ff*
Bath Chronicle, The, 77, 79
Bathwick, 79
Bathwick Hill, 85
Beaminster Manor, Dorset, 14
Beckford, Lady Margaret, née Gordon (wife), 24, 27, 28, 29, 30, 71
Beckford, Louisa, Hon. Mrs. Peter, 19, 24, 25, 26–7, 28, 29
Beckford, Maria, 'the Begum' (mother), 11, 13, 15, 16, 17, 19–20, 24, 25, 28, 30, 71, 118–21
Beckford, Maria Margaret (daughter), *see* Orde, Mrs.
Beckford, Peter (cousin), 19, 24, 26
Beckford, Peter (grandfather), 11
Beckford, Peter (great-grandfather), 11
Beckford, Susan Euphemia (daughter), *see* Hamilton, 10th Duchess of
Beckford, Thomas (great-uncle), 11
Beckford, William, M.P., Alderman (father), 11, 13, 14, 15, 16, 17, 28, 42, 60

'Begum, The', *see* Beckford, Maria
Bellini, Giovanni, 97, 101
Beltz, G. F. (Lancaster Herald), 71
Benett, John, M.P., 76
Bentley, Richard, 110
Berghems, C., 97
Bertoni, F. G., 21, 26
Berwick, (Princess Caroline Stolberg) Duchess of, 35
Biographical Memoirs of Extraordinary Painters, 16, 110
Bitham Lake, Fonthill, 36, 57, 59
Blake, William, 96, 108, 122
Boa Morte Convent, Lisbon, 33
Boboli Gardens, Florence, 56
Bohn, H. G., 104, 105, 106, 107
Boileau, F. J., 15
Bonington, R. P., 96
Borghese Palace, Rome, 65
Borghese, Pauline, Princess, 113
Boys, Thomas Shotter, 96
Brasbridge, J. *(Fruits of Experience)*, 106
Brazil, Prince José of (Regent of Portugal), 38, 43
Brighton Pavilion, 62
Bristol, 4th Earl of and Bishop of Derry, 101
Britton, John *(Illustrations of Fonthill)*, 15, 46, 49, 55, 68, 75, 105
Brockman, H. A. N., 64
Brodick Castle, Buteshire, 73, 113, 116
Bronzino, Angelo, 78
Brown, Lancelot (Capability), 56
Buckler, John, 50, 52
Buhl furniture, 36–7
Bunyan, John, 106
Burlington, 3rd Earl of, 41
Burton, Decimus, 81
Burton, John, 21, 24, 26, 27
Byron, George Gordon, Lord, 7, 26, 73, 107, 110, 118, 121, 122

Canaletto, A., 20
Canterbury, 49
Carency, Prince de, 35
Carter, Elizabeth, 29
Casali, Andrea, 13
Cattermole, George, 52, 96
Cellini, B., 95
Chambers, Sir William, 41
Chapman, Guy, 111
Chardin, Auguste, 37, 105
Chardin, Jean *(Voyage en Perse)*, 25
Charlecote Park, Warwickshire, 64, 66, 68
Chatham, William Pitt, 1st Earl of, 11, 16
Chesterfield, 4th Earl of, 108
Childwall Hall, Leics., 52
Chimène, 21, 22
Christie's, 75
Cimabue, G., 101

Cintra, 38, 106
Cipriani, G. B., 95
Cirencester Park, Glos., 56
Civita Vecchia, 13
Clark, Kenneth (Lord), 42
Clarke, George, 105, 110
Clarke, William, 105
Claude (Le Lorrain), paintings by, 71, 89, 100, 101
Cleveland Bridge, 87
Clogher, Bishop of, 118
Cobbett, William, 52, 92
Coleorton Hall, Leics., 52
Coleridge, S. T., 19
College of Heralds, 71
Combe Down, 77
Coney, John, 96
Constable, John, 52, 96
Contarini Fleming, 26
Corelli, Arcangelo, 20
Cornaro, Catherine, 95
Cornaro family, The, 20
Cosway, Maria, 29
Courtenay, Hon. Charlotte (Lady Loughborough), 18, 28
Courtenay, Hon. William (later 3rd Viscount Courtenay and 9th Earl of Devon), 18–19, 20, 24, 25, 27, 28, 29, 30, 35, 122
Courtenay, 2nd Viscount, 18, 28, 29, 35
Cozens, Alexander, 15–16, 17, 18, 24, 27, 28, 29, 42, 95, 116, 117
Cozens, J. R., 27, 95, 96
Craven, Elizabeth, 6th Lady, Margravine of Anspach, 7, 26, 27, 43
Crome, J. B. (the younger), 96
Crucifixion (style of Orcagna), 97

Damnable Life of Dr. Faustus, The, 106
Dance, George, 81
Daniell, S., 96
Daniell, W., 96
Dante, A., 110
de Cort, Hendrik, 96
Decline and Fall of the Roman Empire, The, 108
Deepdene, The, Surrey, 81
Derome, N.-D., le jeune, 104, 105, 106
Derry, Bishop of, *see* Bristol
Diane de Poitiers, 104
Disraeli, Benjamin, 1st Earl of Beaconsfield, 26, 110
Dixon, John, 49
Don Quixote, 26
Douglas, Marquess of, *see* Hamilton, Alexander
Doyle, John, 92
Dreams, Waking Thoughts and Incidents, 24, 27, 28, 110

Drury Lane, 21, 24
Drysdale, Robert, 13, 31, 36
du Cerceau, J. A., 41
Dulwich College, 81
Dunbar, Mrs. (granddaughter), 73

Eastlake, Sir Charles, 97
Eastnor Castle, Herefordshire, 52
Eaton Hall, Cheshire, 52, 53
Edward III, King, 65, 79
Effingham, Elizabeth 2nd Countess of
    (aunt), 11
Eginton, Francis, and William Raphael, 48,
    60, 62, 68
Eglerton (waiter), 118
Ehrhart, Dr. P. J., 38, 70
Elsheimer, Adam, 57, 59, 98
Ely Cathedral, 64
Embattled Gateway, 87–8, 93
English, E. F., 82, 84, 85, 88, 89, 112–13
Episodes of Vathek, The, 113, 122
Estremadura, Portugal, 56
Etty, William, 96
*Excursion to the Grande Chartreuse in 1778,
    An*, 18
Exhumation of St. Hubert, The, 94, 95

Falmouth, 31
Farinelli, C. B., 21, 22
Farington, Joseph, 8, 36, 42, 44, 71, 110,
    117
Farquhar, John ('Old Filthyman'), 75, 76,
    105
Faust, 26
Fielding, Copley, 96
Finley, W., 52
Firbank, Ronald, 8, 120
Flaxman, John, 15
Florence, 41, 87
Fonthill, Wilts., 11*ff*.
Foxhall & Fryer, 35
Franchi, Gregorio, 34, 36, 38, 42, 47, 49, 64,
    68, 70, 73, 75, 77, 102, 114, 118, 119
Francis I of France, King, 104
Fries, Count, 106
Frith, W. P., 113
Froissart, Jean, 104

Gainsborough, Thomas, 96
Galt, John, 107
Garofolo, B. de, 98, 101
Geneva, 17
Gentleman's Magazine, The, 26, 44, 46, 111
George II, King, 11
George III, King, 11
Germaine, Lady Betty, Margravine of
    Anspach, 95
Giaour, The, 26
Gibbon, Edward, 43, 108
Giotto, 101
Girtin, T., 86
Goodridge, H. E., 79, 80, 82, 85, 86, 102,
    103, 112

Gordon, Jane 4th Duchess of, 100
Gordon, Lady Margaret, *see* Beckford, Lady
    Margaret
Gordon Riots, 20
Gore, Mrs. C. G. F., 114
Grande Chartreuse, The, Dauphiné, 18
Greville, Hon. Charles, 29
Grosvenor, 1st Marquess of, 76

Hadlow Castle, Kent, 52
Hall, T. (*Loathsomeness of Long Haire*), 106
Hamilton, Alexander (afterwards 10th Duke
    of Hamilton), 24, 49, 71, 105, 113, 114,
    117
Hamilton, Archibald, 24
Hamilton, Catherine, Lady, 20, 21, 22, 24,
    27
Hamilton, Charles, (great-uncle), 56, 79
Hamilton, Emma, Lady, 43, 45, 46
Hamilton, Hon. George, M.P.
    (grandfather), 11
Hamilton Palace Sale, 1882–3, 105, 106,
    107, 117
Hamilton, Sir William, 20, 21, 27, 29, 45, 46
Hamilton, Susan Euphemia Beckford, 10th
    Duchess of, 30, 72–3, 105, 113, 116, 117,
    122
Hamilton, 12th Duke of, 105
Hamilton, William, R. A., 48, 62, 71
Hamilton, William Alexander 11th Duke of
    (grandson), 13, 117
Handel, G. F., 27
Harrow School, 25
Harvey, Elizabeth (half-sister), 31
Haydn, J., 20, 34
Hayter, George, 49
Hazlitt, William, 98, 107
Heard, Sir Isaac (Garter King of Arms), 71
Henley, Rev. Samuel, 24, 25, 26, 29, 30
Henri II of France, King, 104
Henry VII, King, 66
Higham, Thomas, 52
Hindon, Wilts., pocket borough, 28, 70, 117
Hinkley Hill, Fonthill, 43
Hoare, James or George, 13, 14, 15
Hoare, Sir Richard Colt, Bt., 101
Hoare, William, 13
Holbein, Hans, 66, 78
Hope, Thomas, 26, 69, 73, 80, 81, 84
Hopper, Thomas, 87
Hoppner, John, 22, 75
Houses of Parliament, 52
Huber, François, 17
Humphrey, Ozias, 71
Hunt, Leigh (*Rimini*), 107

Ibbetson, J. C., 96
Innsbrück, 56
Italy; with Sketches of Spain and Portugal,
    31, 110

James, Sir Walter, 77

John of Gaunt, 65
Johnson, Samuel, 25, 26, 108
Jommelli, N., 20
Jones, Inigo, 13, 14
Jones, Thomas, 27
Journal in Portugal and Spain, The, 31, 32,
    34, 39

Kalthoeber, C. S., 105
Keats, John (*Endymion*), 107
Kensington Palace, 78
Kettle, Tilly, 13

Landor, Walter Savage, 86
Landseer, Sir William, 96
Langhemans, François, 95
Lansdown Cemetery, 115
Lansdown Crescent, Bath, 77 *ff*.
Lansdown Hill, 79, 88
Lansdown, Mr., 54, 85, 88, 89, 90, 92, 103,
    112
Lansdown Tower, Bath, 79 *ff*.
Lausanne, 43
Lawrence, Sir Thomas, 97
Le Brun's *Voyage par la Moscavie, etc.*, 25
Le Keux, John, 52
Le Nozze di Figaro, 20
Lee Priory, Kent, 44, 45
Lettice, Rev. John, 16, 17, 18, 19, 20, 27,
    36, 71
Lewis, Charles, 105–6
Liber Veritatis, 111, 112
Lima, Jeronimo da, 34
Lincoln, Susan Countess of, 113, 117
Lisbon, 31, 32
Lisbon, Beckford's plan of a house at, 39
Lisbon Cathedral (São Vicente), 33, 34
Listenais, Princesse de, 35
Lockhart, J. G., 26, 110, 111
Loudon, J. C., 54, 59
Loughborough, Lord, *see* Wedderburn, A.
Louis XVI of France, King, 37
Loutherbourg, J. P. de, 24, 35, 95
Louvre Palace, Paris, 36, 102
Lowther Castle, Cumb., 52
Lucca, 20, 41
Lyncombe Vale Cemetery, 117, 119
Lysicrates, monument of, 82

Macquin, Abbé, 17, 70
Maddox, Willes, 73, 82, 84, 116, 117
Madrid, 35
Mannheim, 20
Maria I of Portugal, Queen, 32, 38, 40
Marialva, D. Henriqueta, 37
Marialva, Diogo 5th Marquis of, 32, 33, 34,
    37, 106, 122
Marialva, Dom Pedro, 33, 34, 123
Marialva, 'the old [4th] Marquis' (father of
    Diogo), 32–3
Marlborough, 5th Duke of, 104

Martin, Charles, 59
Martin, John, 52, 55
Maslen, B. J., 21
May, Walter Barton, 52
Mazzolini, L., 101
Mélanges Érotiques, etc., 106
Mérigot's bookshop, Paris, 37
Milne (head gardener), 92
Milton, John, 26, 59, 110
Modern Wiltshire (Hoare), plate from, 15
Montagu, Edward Wortley, 104
Montagu, Elizabeth, Mrs., 29
Montagu, Lady Mary W. *(Letters from Turkey)*, 25
Monserrate, Cintra, 38
Moore, J. F., 13–14, 60
Moore, Tom, 73, 113
Morgan, Lady *(Life of Salvator Rosa)*, 107
Morning Herald, The, 29
Morrison family, 76
Mozart, W. A., 20
Munich, 20
Murch, Jerome, 112, 113
Murray, John, 110
Murphy, J. C. *(Plans, Elevations, etc of Batalha)*, 48, 63–4
Musters, Sophia, Mrs., 24
Mysteries of Udolpho, The, 16

Naples, 20, 27
Napoleon I, Emperor, 69, 102, 113
Nash, Beau, 77
Nasmyth, A., 96
National Gallery, 95, 97, 98
National Trust, 23, 96
Neale, J. P. *(Views of Seats)*, 44, 52, 67
Nelson, Horatio, Admiral Viscount, 45, 46
Nemi, Lake (watercolour of), 96
Newstead Abbey, Notts., 73

Oppé, A. E., 16
Orcagna, style of *(Crucifixion)*, 97
Orde, Colonel (later Lieut. General) James, 71
Orde, Margaret Beckford, Mrs., 23, 30, 71, 73, 118
Ossian, 16
Ottley, W. Y., 101
Owen, W., 28

Pacchierotti, G., 20, 21, 22, 24, 26
Padua, 27
Painshill, Surrey, 56
Palazzo Vecchio, 81
Palladio, Andrea, 41
Palmer, John, 77, 79, 103
Palmer, Samuel, 96
Paradise Lost, 26, 59
Paris, 21, 35, 36, 114
Park Street, London (no. 127), 112
Parreaux, André, 18, 26, 120
Penrhyn Castle, Gwynedd, 87

Perro (dwarf), 60, 70, 71
Perugino's *Virgin and Child with St. John*, 101
Peter the Great, 15
Pether, A., 96
Pevsner, Sir Nikolaus, 52
Philip V of Spain, King, 21, 22
Phillips (auctioneers), 76, 113
Pilgrim's Progress, The, 26, 106
Pillement, Jean, 34
Piranesi, G. B., 41
Pisa, 41
Pitt, Hon. George (afterwards 2nd Lord Rivers), 24
Pitt, Hon. William, 43, 70, 117
Pompadour, Madame de, 37
Porden, C. F., 52
Porden, William, 52, 53
Powderham Castle, Devon, 18, 19, 24, 29, 30, 79, 121
Powys, Mrs. Lybbe, 13, 14
Prelude, The, 121
Price, Uvedale *(Essay on the Picturesque, 1794)*, 55, 56–7, 58, 85, 86
Prince Regent (afterwards George IV), The, 62
Prior Park, 77, 87
Prout, S., 96
Pugin, A. W., 41, 52
Pulteney Street, Bath (no. 66), 77
Pythouse, 76

Quarterly Review, The, 26, 110
Queluz Palace, 40
Quevedo, Villegas, 110
Quinta da Ramalhão, Cintra, 34
Quinta dos Bichos, Lisbon, 32, 34, 114
Quinto Fabio, 21

Radcliffe, Ann, Mrs., 16
Raphael, 98, 101, 102
Rasselas, 25, 26
Rauzzini, V., 24
Recollections of an Excursion to the Monasteries of Alcobaça and Batalha, 38, 39, 111
Redding, Cyrus, 71, 85, 101, 104, 112, 113, 122
Rembrandt, 78
Repton, Humphrey, 55
Reynolds, Sir Joshua, 19, 79
Riesener, J. H., 37, 38, 69
Rivers of Stratfieldsaye, 1st Lord, 19
Robinson, P. F., 41
Rogers, Samuel, 65, 71, 110, 113
Rojas, Chevalier de, 35
Rome, 27, 42, 112, 120
Romney, George, 18, 22, 23, 24, 30, 79
Roscoe, William, 101
Rossi, J. C. F., 42, 67, 68
Rosslyn, 1st Earl of, *see* Wedderburn
Roxburghe, 3rd Duke of, sale of collection of, 104

Royal Crescent, Bath, 79
Rubens, Sir P. P., 97
Rushout, Hon. Anne, 15, 17, 75
Rutter, John *(Delineations of Fonthill, 1823)*, 36, 49, 50, 51, 53, 55, 63, 90, 122

Sacchini, A. M. G., 21, 22
St. Antony of Padua, 27, 38, 60, 67, 68, 76, 120, 122
St. Augustine's monastery, Canterbury, 49
St. Cloud, 69
St. Dionysius the Areopagite, 120
St. Peter's, Rome, 42, 121
St. Vincent, 33
Salisbury Cathedral, 52, 120
San Giorgio Maggiore, church of, Venice, 41
Santa Cruz, Marquess of, 35
Saussure, H. Bénédict de, 17
Schöll, Dr. A. F., 43
Scott, Sir Walter, 107–8
Selwyn, George, 22
Shakespeare, William, 110
Shelley, Mary *(Frankenstein)*, 107
Shelley, P. B., 108
Siena, 41
Silva, Polycarpo da, 34
Smith, Charles, 105
Smith, C. Loraine, 22
Smith, John 'Warwick', 70, 96
Smith, Sydney, 120
Soane, Sir John, 15, 81
Sotheby's book sale, July 1966, 104
Sotheby's Hamilton Palace sale, 1882–3, 105, 106
Southey, Robert, 19, 107
Spenser, Edmund, 28
Spinoza, B. de, 121
Stanislaus, King of Poland (bureau), 37, 38
Stolberg, Princess Louise of, 35
Stop Beacon, Fonthill, 42, 43
Storer, James *(A Description of Fonthill)*, 17, 48, 49, 61, 62
Storr, Paul, 87
Stothard, Thomas, 96
Stourhead House, Wilts., 13, 96, 101
Stratton Park, Hants, 81
Stuart, Prince Charles, 35

Tasso, Torquato, 59
Tenducci, G. F., 24
Theakston, Joseph, 60, 76
Thornton, Theophilus, 105
Tiny (Beckford's spaniel), 114, 117
Tintoretto, 97
Titian, 78, 102
Tobias and the Angel, 57, 59
Toddington Manor, Glos., 52
Tresham, Henry, 71
Il Tributo, 24
Turner, J. M. W., 13, 45, 48, 52, 58, 59, 71

Valckenborsch, L. van, 42

Vallière, Duc de la, 104
Van der Weyden, R., 95
Vathek, 7, 14, 24, 25–6, 30, 31, 42, 122
Velasquez, 78
Venice, 20, 27, 41, 42, 102
Verdeil, François, 31, 33
Vernet, A. C. H., 96
Veronese, Paolo, 97
Vevey, Switzerland, 30
Victoria and Albert Museum, 66, 91
Vincent (head gardener), 75, 92–3
Vision, The, 16
Vitruvius, 41
Voltaire, 17
Vyse, Colonel R. H. Howard, *Pyramids of Gizeh*, 107

Waagen, Dr. G. F., 77, 85, 98, 99, 100, 101
Walcot parish, 117
Walcot Poor Rate Book, Bath, 78, 102
Wallace Collection, 37, 66, 67
Walpole, Horace, 8, 11, 42, 56, 114, 116
Walpole, Sir Robert, 32, 34
Wardour Castle, 60
Waterloo, Battle of, 108
Watkin, David, 80, 81
Waugh, Evelyn, 8
Wedderburn, Alexander (Lord Loughborough and 1st Earl of Rosslyn), 20, 28, 29, 30, 70
Wells, Somerset, 29
West, Benjamin, 13, 62, 71, 73
Westminster Abbey, 52, 119
Westminster School, 24

Wild, Charles, 52, 96
Wilde, Oscar, 8
Wildman brothers, 73
Willaume, David, 95
William V, Stadholder, 36
Wilson, John, 106
Wilson, Richard, 96
Witham Abbey, Somerset, 18
Wolsey, Cardinal, 66
Wordsworth, William, 19, 121
Worsley, H. F., 96
Wouvermans, P., 97
Wyatt, James, 7, 15, 42, 43, 44–5, 46, 47, 48, 49, 52, 54, 61, 62, 64–5, 119
Wyatt, Matthew Cotes, 65

Zoffany, J., 20